Integrating Intensive Interaction

This unique book features a collection of lively stories on the integration of Intensive Interaction practice into schools and adult service settings. It addresses communication development, both from a micro and macro level across a variety of service settings, with each chapter written by a different practitioner. These personal accounts cover individual practice and reflection with a single case-study person, as well as influencing organisational change.

The authors assert that, within adult services and educational settings, Intensive Interaction can be used as a way to develop communication and confidence and to work with the principles of inclusion and person-centred acceptance and support. The book develops an understanding of issues that can be addressed within training and mentoring other staff, and uses case studies throughout as a powerful training tool.

Filled with practical advice and techniques to develop communication with people who find it hard to communicate, as well as guidance on ensuring the sustainable extension of the use of Intensive Interaction by embedding the approach within organisational ways of working, this book will be of value to anyone working within children and adult services for people with communication impairments.

Amandine Mourière is a freelance autism and learning disability consultant and an Associate of the Intensive Interaction Institute.

Jules McKim is the Intensive Interaction Coordinator with Oxford Health NHS Foundation Trust and an Associate of the Intensive Interaction Institute.

Integrating Intensive Interaction

Developing Communication Practice in Services for Children and Adults with Severe Learning Difficulties, Profound and Multiple Learning Difficulties and Autism

Edited by Amandine Mourière and Jules McKim

Routledge
Taylor & Francis Group

LONDON AND NEW YORK

First published 2018
by Routledge
2 Park Square, Milton Park, Abingdon, Oxon OX14 4RN

and by Routledge
711 Third Avenue, New York, NY 10017

Routledge is an imprint of the Taylor & Francis Group, an informa business

British Library Cataloguing in Publication Data
A catalogue record for this book is available from the British Library

Library of Congress Cataloging in Publication Data
A catalog record has been requested for this book

ISBN: 978-1-138-10656-7 (hbk)
ISBN: 978-1-138-10657-4 (pbk)
ISBN: 978-1-315-10153-8 (ebk)

Typeset in Bembo
by diacriTech, Chennai

Printed in the United Kingdom
by Henry Ling Limited

This book is dedicated to Dave Hewett, whose passion for teaching and education has empowered practitioners around the world to reach out to children and adults, regardless of their diagnosis or difficulties.

Contents

Figures

Contributors

Cath Brockie is the owner and service provider at Corran Vale, Carmarthenshire, Wales & Corran Dean, Worcestershire, England.

Lucy Golder is a teacher and the Intensive Interaction Co-ordinator at Brimble Hill School in Swindon.

Lucy Hankin is a teaching assistant and an Intensive Interaction Co-ordinator in a special school in the West Midlands catering specifically for pupils with autism.

Kaisa Martikainen is the Development Co-ordinator at the Communication and Technology Centre Tikoteekki and at the The Finnish Association of Intellectual and Developmental Disabilities in Helsinki, Finland.

Jules McKim is the Intensive Interaction Co-ordinator with Oxford Health NHS Foundation Trust and an associate of the Intensive Interaction Institute.

Amandine Mourière is an Autism and Learning Disabilities Consultant, and an associate of the Intensive Interaction Institute.

Michelle Murphy is a Registered Nurse in Intellectual Disability (RNID) and Intensive Interaction Co-ordinator working in Cope Foundation, an Intellectual Disability Service Provider in Ireland. She also delivers guest lectures on Intensive Interaction to BSc Nursing students.

Ben Smith is a Team Leader and Intensive Interaction Co-ordinator in the Positive Behaviour Intervention Service in West Wales.

Pam Smith is a teacher and the Intensive Interaction Co-ordinator at Manor Mead School in Surrey.

Foreword

Dave Hewett

This book lays down another significant waypoint in the roll-out of Intensive Interaction awareness and implementation. It vividly sets out significant descriptions of Intensive Interaction practice development within services and therefore, contributes positively to the further dissemination of the approach. Here, you will find stories that emphasise the way in which Intensive Interaction brings meaningful, vital experiences to a range of people of various needs, impairments and disabilities. You will also find accounts illustrating that the approach can therefore be delivered by various services across the age-range of the people we teach, support and care for.

Intensive Interaction is a pretty unusual animal. I suggest strongly that it should not be unusual, but it is. It is unusual in various respects, but at this moment what I am specifically thinking is this: Intensive Interaction is a practitioner innovation that has gradually become a worldwide dissemination. It was developed quite fully by the team efforts of a bunch of special school classroom staff in the 1980s. The workings of the approach were brought into operation by a combination of practical, sensitive trial and error, and input from the research, then just available, on how people, during infancy, naturally learn to be communicators. The team of which I was a member, judiciously combined the practical and the academic in our development work. As I mention, Intensive Interaction in my view, should not be unusual in this respect of its creation and establishment. Surely, we would all agree that our work should be at all times excitingly moved forward by the regular arising of new developments thoughtfully and methodically produced by practitioners working in the, so to speak, 'front-line'. The fact that this is not the usual state of affairs is an interesting topic that may yet be the focus of a book in its own right.

The first mission of our dissemination has always been the obvious one of making sure of the maximum availability of good Intensive Interaction practice to the people whose lives can be changed by receiving it. Therefore, the dissemination has always been dedicated to helping practitioners to have good technique, to know and assimilate the simple complexities of Intensive Interaction expertise. This effort, led increasingly by experienced practitioners such as Amandine and Jules from our organisation, has always been dedicated to the fullest realisation of this outcome.

'Integrating Intensive Interaction' has arisen from the processes of our Co-ordinator course. The Intensive Interaction Co-ordinator course has become now, a major instrument of our dissemination enterprise. The course is highly practical and practice-oriented, but also includes the full survey of our approach's theoretical underpinnings. We intend to train co-ordinators gradually over about 15 months, intensively and extensively in all the techniques and practices, as well as giving them thorough-going background knowledge, a dedication to and familiarity with reflective practice, practical advice on stimulating organisational and cultural change and preparation in training and mentoring colleagues. We then return to their employing organisation a practitioner who is equipped as a considerable, powerful resource to the organisation.

Amandine Mourière and Jules McKim were prominent members of a dynamic co-ordinator cohort and they are now dedicating their professional lives to the Intensive Interaction mission as associates of our institute. Their group was comprised of a range of potent personalities from a variety of services which even embraced our increasingly international context with two course members from overseas. During the course, participants run projects in their workplaces which have them gradually operating as expert practitioners and then as co-ordinators to their team and workplace. Video evaluations and verbal reports bring their developing stories back to often dynamic seminars as the seven course blocks unfold. As their course reached its final stages, this group agreed that they had created together a significant selection of powerful stories about their experiences of taking Intensive Interaction to their colleagues and services: stories about the rewarding or daunting nature of change within the culture of an organisation, and stories of the power of Intensive Interaction to bring life-changing benefit into the daily experience of some of the most disadvantaged people. They realised and agreed they wanted to record these narratives in the hope of them being of interest and benefit to others who follow.

Thus, for a long time, the working title of this book was: 'Intensive Interaction Co-ordinators: Stories from the front line'. Yes, that's a somewhat silly and over-dramatic title which they are obviously not keeping, but it expressed to me some feeling of the nature of the journeys these nine, earnest, passionate practitioners undertook. In the best Intensive Interaction traditions, this is a book *by* practitioners *for* practitioners. These nine people are practitioners to the core. They care deeply about the welfare of the people they are supporting. They care profoundly about the quality of the services they work within. They have fully demonstrated to themselves the power of Intensive Interaction to change people's lives positively. All these orientations radiate, I suggest, out of the nine chapters in this book.

Dr. Dave Hewett
Director, Intensive Interaction Institute
Malvern, April 2017

Chapter 1

Introduction

Amandine Mourière and Jules McKim

This is a book about nine practitioners, who all went through an individual and professional journey in becoming Intensive Interaction Co-ordinators.

These journeys have been put together as a collection of stories to provide the reader with insight into people's journeys in implementing what they believe in into their service settings. In each chapter, the author tracks their individual use of Intensive Interaction with a single person, their experiences in mentoring other staff, and the initial steps in establishing and embedding Intensive Interaction in their workplaces. With this book, our aim is to share with you a collection of good and lively stories of the development of Intensive Interaction both in school environments and adult residential services.

The approach

Intensive Interaction has been developed and disseminated for over 30 years. As a result, most people in the field of learning disabilities have heard of the approach. However, knowledge of the approach is very different from an understanding of the strategies to develop and establish quality provision of Intensive Interaction. A brief description of the approach is therefore needed for readers who may not be familiar with Intensive Interaction.

Intensive Interaction is an approach for people at early levels of communication development. First and foremost, Intensive Interaction is about spending time with another person, about being connected, and being part of their social world. When we work with people with communication difficulties, our very first goal is to connect with them, to find a way to relate, and eventually empower them to become successful communicators.

> *The essential point here is that 'personal communication is essential for our well-being' and it may be that communication is the 'primary goal' of human existence.* (Adler & Rodman, 2006).

Intensive Interaction promotes social inclusion by teaching the pre-speech fundamentals of communication (Nind & Hewett, 2001). It is used with children and adults who have severe learning difficulties and/or autism and adults with dementia.

The fundamentals of communication

- enjoying being with another person
- developing the ability to attend to that person
- concentration and attention span
- learning to do sequences of activity with another person
- taking turns in exchanges of behaviour

- sharing personal space
- using and understanding eye contact
- using and understanding facial expressions
- using and understanding physical contacts
- using and understanding non-verbal communication
- using vocalisations with meaning
- learning to regulate and control arousal levels

The teaching of these fundamentals takes place in the most naturalistic and humanistic ways, through daily interactions. As the people supporting an individual become more confident as practitioners, Intensive Interaction becomes an integral and essential part of their social-communication fabric.

Intensive Interaction stems from the natural model of communication learning, and therefore borrows some key principles from the parent-infant model of interaction. Holding back, observing and waiting are key in empowering an individual to take the first turn, and to therefore become a fully active participant in the interaction. By tuning-in, the practitioner can then time their responses to effectively support the flow of the interaction. Being relaxed and unhurried is essential; it allows for the pace to be dictated by the person, and thus be just right for them. Through bursts of active periods, the person may need time to process what has just happened, or to rest. This time is called a 'pause,' and will be as long and as frequent as the person needs it to be. All the while, the practitioner remains tuned-in, with an available look and body language, responsive in stand-by. Responses can be as varied and unique as people are: imitating, modified reflecting, gentle dramatisations, marking what the person did using facial expressions and body language, delighted face/voice, bursts of speech or running commentary.

How is Intensive Interaction being disseminated?

The principles and techniques of Intensive Interaction are so natural, that some people can grasp enough after a one-day course to become practitioners.

The Intensive Interaction Institute offers however a range of courses available to practitioners and parents, from a 1-day introductory course, a 3-day good practice course to a 21-day course. The latter is the Co-ordinators' Course, and is the most complete and in-depth course the Institute offers. It takes place over a period of 15 months, and is split into 7 blocks of 3 days. This format allows practitioners time to develop their practice. Practice is a key element in the completion of the course, but other aspects of becoming a co-ordinator are taken into consideration: understanding the rationale underpinning Intensive Interaction, the ability to mentor colleagues as well as to deliver workshops and training within their organisations, influencing organisational change and development. The course includes seminars on autism, parent-infant interactions, the use of physical contact, challenging behaviours, organisational issues, etc.

Co-ordinators are usually highly motivated individuals who are chosen by their organisations to be trained, and eventually disseminate and embed the approach themselves in their settings.

Why this book?

The idea of a collective book came in April 2015, on the final block of this particular Co-ordinators' Course. The format of this course is very unique, and gives amazing opportunities to develop a professional network. The course takes place over a period of 16 months and requires each participant to select an individual they have regular access to, in order to record and assess the individual's progress as well as providing opportunities for the practitioner to reflect on their own practice and develop accordingly. On the last block, each course member presents a summary of their project which showcases the journey and change that has taken place for each individual. On the last day of the last block, we were all sitting around the big table for lunch (about 12 of us). Whilst all very pleased with the thought of becoming fully-fledged co-ordinators, there was a heavy feeling of sadness in the air. We were all very aware that this was the end of a rather exceptional adventure together. What is more, it felt like a shame that these incredible journeys we all went through with our person, as well as with our organisation, would end like this. Someone, Michelle I think, jokingly suggested that we write a collective book. Soon, everyone started to warm up to the idea, and before we had time to process, both Jules and I were designated to be the editors.

Outline of chapters

In chapter 2, Pam relates her Intensive Interaction journey with five-year-old Hayden, a boy who was more interested in shiny beads than in people. With warmth and great passion, Pam tells us how she raised Intensive Interaction's profile in her school, and enthused her colleagues to subsequently create an Intensive Interaction Club. She also writes about the inclusion of Intensive Interaction within Education, Health and Care Plans (EHCPs) and the importance of ensuring communication work is not reduced to SMART targets (Specific, Measurable, Attainable, Relevant and Time-framed).

In chapter 3, Jules gives us an account of his Intensive Interaction journey with Dennis, a middle-aged man with severe learning disabilities in a supported living setting. Jules also gives us a valuable insight into his already established Intensive Interaction co-ordinator role, and developing and expanding that role when his Trust was acquired by a much larger NHS Trust.

In chapter 4, Michelle relates her journey with John, who blossomed through the use of Intensive Interaction. Michelle talks with great enthusiasm about the simplicity of Intensive Interaction, and yet the crucial impact it has on communication and well-being. She also makes reference to attachment theory and Maslow's hierarchy of needs in order to promote the role of social interactions within the provision of adult residential services.

Chapter 5 focusses primarily on the importance of minimalism. Amandine explains how Sarah helped her rethink her understanding of Intensive Interaction techniques. By doing less, not only did she see Sarah's communication develop greatly, but she also became a better mentor for her colleagues. Amandine also includes in-depth detail from the recording processes she followed that beautifully illustrates reflective practice in action.

In chapter 6, it is with great passion and conviction that Lucy tells us how her practice developed hand in hand with Vincent's gradual abilities to connect with her. She talks with clarity about her journey to deepen her understanding of Intensive Interaction, and then to expand the knowledge and use of the approach within her school environment.

Chapter 7 gives an invaluable understanding of the crucial importance of using video in mentoring. Kaisa describes in great detail how she mentored a support staff member to carry out Intensive Interaction with Laura. Informed by Video Interaction Guidance, Kaisa's sensitive and empowering mentoring style is illustrated with transcripts of conversations she had with her mentees.

In chapter 8, Cath gives a precious account of how to successfully embed Intensive Interaction into a service's ethics. Cath movingly recalls her journey with John, an adult with severe learning disabilities and behaviours that services found challenging and how Intensive Interaction changed his life. As CEO of her provider organisation she explains how Intensive Interaction has become the core of her services' DNA.

In chapter 9, Lucy relates her sensitive journey with Logan, and how he learnt to express his emotions to ultimately find comfort in others. The development of Intensive Interaction in her school began as an almost 'underground movement' but with great strength and persistence, Lucy has made it mainstream.

In chapter 10, Ben discloses with humble honesty how Intensive Interaction made him re-evaluate and change his practice from one focussing on behavioural modification to now focussing on relationships and emotional well-being. His biggest learning opportunity was presented to him under the name of Mick, and Ben recalls how he had to learn to do less, in order to let Mick do more.

It is hoped that these stories will affect people differently in a very positive and uplifting way. For those who are new to Intensive Interaction, or perhaps know a little of the approach already, we hope to inspire you to find out more, and try it for yourself. For those of you who are already practitioners and great believers of the approach's benefits, these stories will hopefully encourage you to keep faith, to stay strong and remind you that if you have passion, it only takes one person to start a movement in the right direction.

References

Adler, R. B. and Rodman, G. R. (2006) *Understanding Human Communication*. 9th edn. New York, NY: Oxford University Press.

Nind, M. and Hewett, D. (2001) *A Practical Guide to Intensive Interaction*. Kidderminster, UK: British Institute of Learning Disabilities.

Chapter 2

Becoming the beads

An Intensive Interaction journey with Hayden

Pam Smith

Pam relates her Intensive Interaction journey with five-year-old Hayden, a boy who was more interested in shiny beads than in people. With warmth and passion, Pam tells us how she raised Intensive Interaction's profile in her school, and enthused her colleagues to subsequently create an Intensive Interaction (II) Club. She also writes about the inclusion of Intensive Interaction within EHCPs and the importance of ensuring communication work is not reduced to an objectives driven exercise.

Introducing Hayden

In the centre of the classroom, Hayden sits on the floor absorbed in twiddling a string of shiny beads. He watches them intently as they twirl back and forth apparently oblivious to his surroundings. Around him, Hayden's classmates are busy playing or moving around the classroom. Occasionally, Hayden glances up but is quickly re-captivated by the sparkly hypnotic motion. For him, everything else fades into the background. Left alone he is happy in his 'bubble' – Hayden and his precious beads.

Hayden attends a special school for children with severe learning difficulties, complex needs and autism. He started at the primary school two years ago and is now five years old. Hayden has a diagnosis of tuberous sclerosis and severe learning difficulties. His medical condition impacts upon his ability to learn, he has social communication difficulties and severe epilepsy. Hayden's seizures have a significant and detrimental effect on his health and well-being. Unfortunately, when Hayden is especially lively it can be a precursor to a seizure. So if he has a day when he is particularly 'switched on,' happy and motivated, this is often followed a few hours later by a large seizure. Hayden is always left drained and exhausted following this, and needs a considerable amount of time (sometimes several days) to get back to his usual cheery self. At these times, he tends to retreat to a cosy corner in his classroom where he curls up and rests, emerging for snacks, play and to participate in short bursts of activities with adult encouragement and support.

Why choose Hayden?

At the start of the project Hayden was quite self-contained, self-absorbed and often seemed isolated. He did not spontaneously seek out adults or peers and his play tended to be repetitive, centring upon sprawling on a huge shiny metal hemisphere in the playground, and twiddling his shiny beads or exploring sensory trays in the classroom. People appeared to have little importance to Hayden unless they could provide him with food or things that he wanted. Having said this, he definitely had favourite adults who had worked with him for several years and his face would light up if they initiated a game or a hug. This contrast between isolation and connectedness suggested that Hayden had the desire to communicate but had not yet learnt the skills to do so, indicating that he would be an ideal candidate for Intensive Interaction.

Hayden has a calm demeanour and is generally a cheerful, affectionate, engaging little boy. He is very motivated by food, tickles and shiny or spinning objects. Hayden is pre-verbal and makes his needs known by taking an adult by the hand and leading them to what he wants (often the cupboard where the snacks are kept!). He is able to communicate his feelings at a simple level – he smiles when happy, cries if unhappy and will sometimes scream or bite his hand if frustrated. Hayden needs plenty of time to process information.

Hayden's previous Intensive Interaction experience

I first met Hayden while he was still in the nursery. At this time, he was enjoying Intensive Interaction with his two highly skilled nursery teachers and also with his classroom assistants – all of whom adopted the approach following whole-school training with Dave Hewett several years previously. Hayden responded well to these sessions, but videos suggest (and his staff agree in retrospect!) that activities tended to be initiated and led by the adults consisting of games such as 'Row the Boat,' action rhymes, and chase and tickle games.

While in the nursery, Hayden was very responsive if an adult bounced him on their knee, played a familiar game or sang his favourite songs (e.g. 'Jelly on a Plate' or 'I'm a Wobbly Man'). There is some great video footage of him at this time, giggling and responding, but he does not initiate interactions and waits passively for the adult to make the first move. This passivity was exacerbated by Hayden's interest in his special objects (keys, beads, fluffy keyrings, jingly toys) and his ability to focus upon them single-mindedly to the exclusion of everything else around him.

Choosing Hayden for the project

The Intensive Interaction Co-ordinator's training course requires each participant to work with an individual and track their progress over the period of a year. Videos and detailed recording sheets charting the individual's progress are shared and evaluated at each training block, held at roughly six-week intervals. The course participants are encouraged to use a combination of expert tutor advice, peer feedback and self-reflection to examine and improve their practice. Their learning journey is underpinned by the knowledge gained from tasks and areas of study covered by the course. The process is very supportive and encouraging whilst still providing critical and detailed evaluation. This enables participants to move forward with their individuals and gain confidence while constantly looking for ways to improve their own practice.

When I began my Intensive Interaction Co-ordinator's training course in March 2014, Hayden was an obvious candidate for my project. My choice was influenced by several factors. Firstly, we were encouraged by our tutors not to choose the most difficult to reach person for this project so that we could practice our skills and hopefully see some progress. Hayden had no significant behavioural issues and was a delight to work with, so this box was well and truly ticked! Secondly, Hayden had previously experienced Intensive Interaction and, as stated above, seemed to enjoy social interaction but lacked the skills to seek it out. I felt learning and practicing these skills would enhance Hayden's quality of life, improve his well-being and ability to learn so this also supported my choice. Finally, I knew that Hayden's family (especially his Mum) were desperate for meaningful ways of communicating with him and helping him to communicate with them, and would support the practice at home as would his class team. After discussion with our headteacher, Hayden's parents and class teacher, it was agreed that he was an ideal choice. The necessary permissions were obtained and times arranged for regular sessions.

Setting up the project

At this time, I was employed part time by the school to work with pupils who needed extra support, including Hayden. The headteacher was very supportive of the course and agreed to my working individually with Hayden in the soft playroom for three half-hour sessions each week. There are arguments for and against this arrangement. Ideally, Intensive Interaction should take place 'any time, any place, anywhere' (Hewett, 2015), giving opportunities for small bursts of communication and special moments that happen naturally within each day to be grasped and developed. However, due to my other commitments there had to be a compromise.

On a positive note, this arrangement offered three substantial, distraction-free chunks of time with Hayden. Also, returning to the same environment enabled Hayden to learn over time that 'this is what we do' in soft play. The downside was that Hayden was not always in the mood! For example, originally two sessions were held during lunchtime play and a third in the late morning. This latter session was quickly rearranged to an early morning slot as Hayden was ravenous by 11:30am and more focused on getting to the Hall for dinner than coming to soft play for Intensive Interaction! This was a good reminder about Maslow's Hierarchy of Needs (Maslow, 1943) and I quickly learnt that for Hayden to be at his most communicative he needed to have a full tummy, be well-rested, comfortable, and in a good frame of mind.

As time went on we did not always work in soft play, sometimes staying in class or moving out to the playground. This protected time was extremely valuable, however, and ensured that Hayden had opportunities to participate regularly in Intensive Interaction.

Observation and suitability of Intensive Interaction as an approach

I had been working with Hayden before I started the course, but the project enabled me to focus on him in a way that I had not done previously. Before starting the training course, we were asked to carry out observations and film videos of the chosen individual to act as a baseline. This observation video (described at the start of this chapter), showed Hayden to be quite oblivious to his classmates and very focussed on his special object – his shiny beads.

On the first block of the course, we watched this video and everyone agreed on two things. Firstly, that Hayden was absolutely gorgeous (which everyone at our school already knew!) and secondly, whatever he was getting from his beads was more motivating than interacting with the people around him.

What's so great about Hayden's beads?

During the course our group was shown video footage of a young man called John. He was one of the first individuals Dave Hewett, Melanie Nind and their colleagues had worked with using Intensive Interaction. John had a yellow rattle that he used as a 'flappy' or self-stimulating object. The yellow rattle was the centre of John's universe and far more motivating for him than human interaction. Following the video, we sat and analysed why John was so motivated by this object and what purpose it might fulfil for him. Watching John, I was immediately struck by the similarity with Hayden's situation. I began to think of the 'flappies' and special objects that had been the focus of the many young people that I had worked with, and tried to envisage what made these preferable to human contact.

As a group, we started suggesting ideas of what John was getting from his yellow rattle. These included:

— *Interesting*
— *Sameness/familiarity*
— *Predictable*
— *Right tempo*
— *Just enough stimulation*
— *He was in control*
— *He could take a break when he wanted*
— *Right pace*
— *Uncomplicated*
— *He could understand what was going on*

Dave Hewett then pointed out that reversing this list provided insight into the things that might make it hard for John to want to interact with us:

Yellow rattle	Other people can be...
Interesting	Not as interesting as special object
Sameness/familiarity	Changeable/unfamiliar
Predictable	Unpredictable
Right tempo	Can get the tempo wrong
Just enough stimulation	Can over- or under-stimulate
He was in control	Take over control
He could take a break when he wanted	Don't give breaks
Right pace	Can get the pace wrong
Uncomplicated	Too complicated/complex
He could understand what was going on	Not easy to understand

Figure 2.1 John's exercise.

These key points were indicators of how we could modify our behaviour to be more accessible. They were also food for thought regarding how we could change our ways of interacting to give back control to individuals who find communicating a challenge. Armed with this knowledge, I started to think about how I could shape my interactions with Hayden to make myself more accessible to him. My mission was to become more like his beads!

Becoming the beads

Intensive Interaction is based upon the natural model of learning communication. It follows the same patterns experienced by typically developing babies who learn to communicate through interacting with their caregivers. The research literature in this field shows that caregiver/infant interaction is hugely enjoyable for both parties as they take an interest in, are delighted by, and get to know each other (Nind and Hewett, 2006). The adult celebrates and encourages every response from the baby, following their lead, tuning-in and continually reinforcing their attempts at communicating. This is achieved through copying their sounds and actions, joining in and using exaggerated, delighted facial expressions, voice and body language.

Videos of caregiver/infant interaction show clearly that the baby always leads the communication 'dance' and the adult is constantly watching them; alert and ready, pausing and waiting for them to do the next thing that they can reflect back. The adult's watchfulness and sensitivity leads to the tempo and content of the interaction being right for the baby. The behaviour of the adult is also more understandable as it becomes simplified and pared back to basics, so that the baby is not overwhelmed (Hewett, 2012a).

The adult, as the more skilled communicator, continually adapts their behaviour to encourage and support the baby's communication and the relationship develops through many tiny moments of connectedness into longer and more complex exchanges. Gradually the adult may introduce running commentary and extend games. They remain continually mindful of the baby's experience and wellbeing, scaffolding the development of the interplay of dynamic human connectedness at the infant's tempo. These principles underpin the work of the communicative partnership in Intensive Interaction (Nind and Hewett, op. cit.).

Tracking Hayden's progress

A combination of session notes and video observations were used to compile the following narrative. The accompanying video shows examples of Hayden's progress but not every aspect mentioned below was captured on film. This again reflects the reality of not always having a spare member of staff available to video the session, and the challenge of videoing solo when working with a child who moves around and grabs the camera when it is set up ready to record!

Early sessions – March and April 2014

The biggest challenge of using Intensive Interaction with Hayden was his passivity and (to put it bluntly) lack of interest in me. As stated previously, Hayden can be very self-contained and self-absorbed and when we first started work together he had some very ritualistic play involving his feet. He is a very sensory boy and these foot games comprised of him dribbling on his toes and stroking or mouthing them. Once engaged in this it was quite difficult to know if he had even noticed me sitting with him, let alone realised that I was there to play!

I began to understand that this was probably why previous work on Intensive Interaction had been so adult-led and was tempted to start making sounds, singing his favourite songs, tapping surfaces and generally jumping around to attract his attention. However, armed with the background reading and support from the course I tried to hold firm and wait for his first move. I waited … and waited … and waited … for what seemed like an eternity. Hayden had found a spot where he felt comfortable on the wall of the ball pond, and I positioned myself below him. Eventually it paid off. Hayden made eye contact. It was fleeting but it was there. He stepped down and turned to the wall and started to rock back and forth. I copied him alongside and he tolerated me in his space for a few seconds and then beetled off to another area. We were up and running!

As March progressed Hayden's eye contact remained fleeting but occurred more frequently. He would snatch glances at me seeming to say 'Are you still here?' and then carry on with his foot games or curl up into a ball on the wall. By the end of March, he started to make 'sss' sounds and looked at me when I copied him. He then started to vocalise 'oh' and 'uh' and made eye contact when I joined in. He held his foot out and I blew raspberries on it and pretended to nibble his toes while saying 'num num num'. Joining in with his preference for foot games worked really well and he started holding up his foot to request more. At this point, Hayden needed lots of breaks and much of my time was spent being quiet and still, waiting for him to be ready for the next game.

In April, Hayden moved away from the ball pond wall and went to the trampette (small trampoline). He really seemed to like the scratchy sounds he could make on the surface with his fingernails. Hayden listened intently when I joined in and then started to take turns. Hayden scratched, then stopped and listened to me. When I stopped he would start again. Over the next few sessions he experimented with making different sounds on the canvas. Each time he listened intently to check that I was following him, smiling when he recognised his sounds and actions being reflected back.

Some new vocalisations emerged this month. These included lip smacking, tongue clicks, 'bee', 'tchtch', 'buh'. Most significantly Hayden started to put syllables together – 'buhbuhbuh-buh'. Hayden's eye contact was not yet sustained but when he got excited and initiated a chase game, he used it meaningfully, looking behind to check I was following. Two new activities emerged this month – Hayden's hopping up and down 'happy' movement and rolling on a soft cylinder shape. He started to get the idea that I was there to interact and was becoming more experimental and confident in his play. The dribbling on his feet stopped but he still curled up in a ball when he needed to take a break.

Progress and cautionary tales – May and June 2014

During May I took some more observation videos of Hayden in the playground, and noticed him looking around and taking more of an interest in his surroundings. He now moved away from his favourite silver hemisphere to investigate other areas of the playground, even though it remained very attractive for him. Our sessions in soft play continued much as before with a combination of scratching games on the trampette, chase games and exploring equipment.

In June, Hayden brought a favourite toy (set of keys) to the session. I unwisely tried to remove these from him and put them on a high shelf but his awareness of object permanence was clearly demonstrated when he spent much of the session climbing up to get them! He was not happy and the interaction stalled. When he brought his keys again next session I decided to go with the flow, working with him and the toy rather than taking it away. The session was more successful and it became apparent that although Hayden wanted his toy, he would put it down for short periods and become more focussed on our interaction. He would then return to the toy when he wanted a break. Over the next few weeks some new vocalisations emerged, including 'bimbim', 'yeah', 'deedoo', 'pop', 'hee', 'huh', 'uh lo' (which I responded to with "hello"), and also some gorgeous smiles.

At this point I felt the pressure of having to share videos at the next training block, and became anxious that Hayden was not moving on quickly enough: perhaps I was not being interesting enough and our play was too repetitive. I attempted introducing a game of 'Round the Garden,' having been told that he had responded well to this when an adult played it with him in class. My attempt failed miserably and Hayden appeared confused about why I was suddenly imposing something on him. He was singularly unimpressed, disengaged and moved away. There were many learning points from this experience. Firstly, that I had to let the process work without taking control. Secondly, that Hayden needed to repeat activities many times and would adapt or modify his responses subtly over time, and naturally without my interference. Thirdly, that you don't need to finish a rhyme! By the time I was half way through, Hayden was obviously not responding but I still soldiered on to the end … Why?? Needless to say, when it's not working just stop – the nursery rhyme police won't arrest you!

When I showed my video, the critical feedback was that I was doing too much, getting in his face and crowding him. In my anxiety to move him on, I was shadowing him constantly in case I missed something, not giving him space to move away and come back in his own time. My colleagues encouraged me to relax, give Hayden time and space, and trust that if he was enjoying the interaction he would return. This was to prove absolutely true. My positive feedback was 'don't fix what isn't broken' as the rest of the group could see Hayden was making lovely progress. I resolved to do less, to embrace minimalism and the most vital learning of all – to have NO AGENDA and NO EXPECTATIONS when starting a session. As one of our colleagues from the group was fond of saying: 'Things are as they are.' That became my Intensive Interaction mantra.

July 2014

During July I tried to apply the feedback suggestions from the group and pared my practice right back. As predicted the sessions became much richer. Hayden's vocalisations started becoming louder and clearer. There were no new sounds but his 'buhbuh', 'uh', 'ah' and 'oh-oh' seemed much more confident and Hayden started to look at me when he vocalised, expecting me to join in and smiling when I did so.

Moving on – September and October 2014

Hayden's health wasn't great when he returned to school after the summer break, and we had several sessions when our time together was just spent lying down next to each other in his comfy corner in the classroom, sharing space. During these times, he often reached out to hold my hand and kept hold of it even when it looked as if he was sleeping. When I went to take my hand away to leave him to rest he tightened his grip as if to encourage me to stay close. This was a real privilege. Hayden was gaining comfort from another person rather than his special objects. This seemed a huge step forward.

There were several similar sessions both in class and soft play during which I remained very quiet but close and joined in with any of Hayden's behaviours that I felt were intentional communication. This included a foot tapping game I extended by tapping on his back and vocalising gently, which made him smile. When I was not sure if Hayden wanted to be with me, I reminded myself that he had the whole of the classroom or soft play to go to if he wanted to move away, but he chose to stay in close physical contact.

In October Hayden's health improved and our sessions became more animated. One particularly special interaction happened out in the playground. Hayden suddenly jumped up from playing on his beloved silver hemisphere and ran away, looking over his shoulder to see if I was chasing him. As he ran, Hayden said 'teagle' (his version of 'tickle'). I chased and tickled Hayden and he laughed. Hayden then approached another member of staff in the playground to engage her in playing. Hayden was now able to initiate an interaction with other adults rather than waiting to be approached to play a game. This was a real cause for celebration!

November and December 2014

During November Hayden became much more comfortable with face to face interaction. His eye contact became more sustained; he started looking at facial expressions and noticed when I copied him. One of his favourite actions at this time was blowing out his cheeks and making a raspberry sound with his lips. He found it very funny when I copied this and pushed my cheeks.

Hayden's new vocalisations during November included 'deedah', 'didikaa', 'dinner', 'tickle', 'mum mum mum' and 'uhuhuhuhuh'. He was giggling and smiling more and showing a real increase in his expressive facial language. He also showed some signs of shared attention for the first time, looking at the twinkly lights in the soft play den, looking at me when I said and signed "lights" and then looking back at the lights. He also touched the large ball, looked at me when I said and signed 'buh buh buh ball' then looked back at the ball and vocalised 'buh buh buh' shortly afterwards. Although this only happened once, Hayden seemed to be starting to associate sounds with his special objects, for example saying 'kuh' when he held the keys. Hayden initiated 'Row the Boat' for the first time this month, sitting on my lap and rocking backwards and forwards then side to side. When I stopped, Hayden rocked again and held out his hands to indicate he wanted more.

The most exciting development in November was a mini-conversation after lunch one day. Hayden said 'Dinner,' I responded 'Dinner?' and Hayden smiled and replied 'Num num num'. When I mentioned this to his class teacher she confirmed that it had been one of Hayden's favourite dinners and was indeed yummy!

There were some more magic moments in December. I went to meet Hayden in class one day as he was finishing lunch. He happily shared his space with me and greeted me with lots of smiles and vocalisations, saying 'num num num' and then playing with his hand over his mouth making 'wah wah' sounds. While eating, Hayden looked around the room watching the children and adults. He seemed much more interested in people and engaged with his surroundings.

By this time, Hayden was consistently requesting 'tickle' and would repeat his request up to three times in a session making great eye contact. He also said 'go' and we played 'Ready Steady Go' anticipation and tickle games which caused great giggles. Hayden still had days when he was less responsive and more reflective following illness or seizures. On these occasions, I gave him space and he often came up and sat on my lap for a hug.

Enriching the relationship – January and February 2015

Prior to January 2015, Hayden had seemed to associate me just with our 1:1 sessions and didn't appear to acknowledge me elsewhere. However, after the Christmas holidays I was interacting with another child in his class when he came up on two occasions, grinned and gave me a large hug. In soft play, he developed a new game of bouncing up and down on the trampette, saying 'oh oh oh,' making sustained eye contact and giggling when I joined in. He also encouraged a game of 'buzzing' his neck by snuggling in, waiting for the 'buzz', turning away and then looking over his shoulder, grinning and making eye contact to indicate he wanted more. This was a great example of Hayden using eye contact and body language to communicate and it was great to see him using both in combination!

Continuing games included chase and tickle, rough and tumble, tapping on big and small physio balls, blowing raspberries, squeezing or tickling his feet, and scratching the canvas on the trampette. New games this month included 'Piggy went to Market' and going up and down the slide, encouraging me to follow. New sounds included 'gooh' (good?) and 'ahden' (Hayden?). Although Hayden sometimes brought toys to sessions, he quickly put them down and was more motivated by the interaction. People were becoming more interesting than beads! This was clearly shown when he abandoned his fluffy key ring one day to initiate a ten-minute sequence of hugs, tickles and cuddles, returning for more each time I disengaged!

In February, for the first time, Hayden walked independently to the soft play room, cued only by the photo (until this point he had walked with me, holding my hand). Hayden was now using longer sequences of sounds more purposefully (seven syllables of 'buh', 'um', and 'muh (more?).' His vocalisations were starting to have a babbling quality with elongated vowels so that his sounds were more 'wordlike' (e.g. 'baaa' rather than 'buh'). Hayden initiated 'Jelly on a Plate' by sitting on my lap and jiggling up and down, and gave a big grin when I sang the song and requested it several more times.

Hayden became interested in a running commentary linked to his actions and looked at me and grinned when I said "Jumping, Hayden's jumping." In February, Hayden also acknowledged me for the first time when walking down the corridor after getting off his bus, smiling and making direct eye contact.

March and April 2015

By March, Hayden was starting to play with sounds. For example, when he had a cold he loved the 'ungah' sounds his blocked nose enabled him to make! New sounds included 'tuh', 'gogogogo' and 'nahnahnah'. Old favourite games still continued, but for the first time I saw Hayden looking at himself in the mirror and watching as he made different facial expressions and looking at my face reflected behind him. The quality of Hayden's touch changed, and he now hugged me and touched my face with great tenderness, and sometimes held my face in both hands, gazing into my eyes. This was a moment of real emotional connectedness and felt incredibly special!

Hayden's motivation for Intensive Interaction was clearly shown in March when I arrived one day and found he had already gone out to play. Thinking it was going to be tricky to encourage him to leave his favourite shiny hemisphere, I showed him the soft play photograph expecting him to ignore me. Instead he immediately got up and ran to the soft play room, checking over his shoulder that I was following! Throughout this month, we continued playing the same old favourite games. Hayden also developed a new game of bouncing on the physio ball, tapping and vocalising to request more.

During April, the final project month, Hayden did nothing new or dramatic. This reflects the nature of development typified by Intensive Interaction which Hewett likens to a spiral which can go up, down, broaden or stay static rather than a tidy, linear progress (Hewett, 2012b). Hayden continued to enjoy our games and practiced his skills by repeating his favourite activities again and again. However, the quality of the interaction was unique each time and never got stale. He had some quiet days following seizures and other more lively days when he showed his cheeky personality and we had a lot of fun. The connectedness remained the most special aspect of the interaction together with Hayden's affectionate use of touch, which sometimes seemed to indicate 'I'm just going over there for a minute but I will be back' (shown in the last video clip).

Continuing and developing Intensive Interaction at our school

Part of the Co-ordinator's Course involved finding ways of making Intensive Interaction more visible around the school and developing the innovations that we had begun into sustainable practice in our establishments.

We were each tasked with taking on a mentee to work with. I was lucky enough to have three colleagues who wanted to train as mentees: Dana, Angela and Felicity. We started meeting weekly to discuss Intensive Interaction theory and practice, complete workbooks and review and evaluate videos of their work. These videos were then brought to the course to be discussed by the group and feedback was shared with the trio, who would use it to inform, adapt and improve their practice.

The quality of their work was outstanding and their enthusiasm was incredible. I will never forget when Dana chased me down the corridor to announce 'Owen (her project child) laughed!' We hugged and Dana cried! This was typical of the commitment of all three mentees and the delight they took in telling me about the amazing transforming power of Intensive Interaction with their children. To do this justice would take a separate chapter of its own. The mentees were awarded their certificates of achievement in front of the whole school during a staff training day. Dana told me that apart from giving birth it was the proudest day of her life!

As the weeks went by, other members of staff started noticing our meetings and asked if they could join us. Before long we had formed an Intensive Interaction Club of around nine staff members representing classes from each key stage, which now meets weekly after school. We share chocolate biscuits, watch, discuss and evaluate videos and talk about their experience of Intensive Interaction with their students during the previous week. Each tiny step of progress is celebrated and applauded. The club has really helped to raise the profile of Intensive Interaction throughout the school and is also great fun.

The members of the club are fantastic! They give up their time every week willingly and enthusiastically, as they are all deeply committed to Intensive Interaction and its ability to connect to the most difficult to reach children and young people. They have helped me create a photo display showing Intensive Interaction in action, have generously shared videos of their work for use when training parents, and most recently played a major role in a whole staff training session in which each person shared their videos and explained what Intensive Interaction meant to them and the children with whom they worked. Several members of the group had never done anything like this and some had never spoken in public before. But their commitment to Intensive Interaction is such that they gladly participated and did a fabulous job. The headteacher commented that this was one of the most inclusive pieces of staff training that the school has ever had. We have been invited back to give termly updates.

Looking to the future

In February 2015, we included an Intensive Interaction Communication target in Hayden's Individual Education Plan (IEP). We have great support from and work closely with our Speech and Language Therapists, notably Sheena Marie Worsfold, and the agreed wording was: '*To continue to develop Hayden's communication through Intensive Interaction, working towards increasing the frequency and diversity of his vocalisations and increasing his initiation of communication.*' The issue of how to include Intensive Interaction as a target has been considered a number of times at school (notably when setting objectives for the new Education Health and Care Plans). The main concern is how best to phrase these targets while still maintaining the integrity of Intensive Interaction as an 'outcome led not target driven' holistic process (Hewett, 2015). There is always a risk that including Intensive Interaction on an IEP or as a learning objective will lead to people having an agenda during the sessions and trying to measure progress against SMART targets (specific, measurable, agreed upon, realistic and time-framed). As Mark Barber recently challenged at the 2015 Intensive Interaction Conference UK – do we really only value things that can be measured? This is a continuing area of discussion for us as a school, as we get to grips with the new paperwork, explore ways of integrating the use of video to show progress and begin to use our II Club meetings for peer moderation in line with Barber's recommendations (Barber, 2012).

In order to capture new developments in Intensive Interaction we have been testing the FOCAL (Fundamentals of Communication Assessment and Learning) Pilot Pack. This system, devised by Amandine Mourière (2015) is proving extremely valuable, enabling us to capture progress not shown in P Levels or Key Skills recording and share it with new staff when children move to new classes or schools to ensure continuity.

We have also started to explore using Intensive Interaction with children who have functional language and can talk about their specialist interests at great length but who struggle with social interaction. This exciting area has resulted in a mini study which shows significant improvement in the individual pupils' social skills. It will be continued next year with more children to assess the impact across this population of more verbal students.

Continuing work with Hayden

Although the project has finished, my sessions with Hayden have continued, shaped according to how he is on the day and what he chooses to do. Some days Hayden gets into Intensive Interaction mode very quickly and is raring to go. Other days it can take up to ten minutes of sitting and waiting quietly while he settles and is ready to interact. Hayden's vocalisations continue to develop and extend and he is now playing with sounds, discovering how to 'wibble' his lip and 'chatting' or vocalising pretty much constantly throughout sessions, combining up to eight syllables at a time. What a huge step forward from the tentative 'uh' and 'sss' of his early sessions. Hayden has found his voice!

Being the beads

Hayden has also discovered that people can be more fun than a silver hemisphere or a string of beads and I now see him around the school, interacting with his lovely class staff, initiating games, making meaningful eye contact, smiling, giggling and snuggling in for cuddles. We have learnt how to communicate in a way that is accessible for Hayden and he has blossomed in response to this and is following us into the wider world of communication. Hopefully, Hayden, we have become your beads.

References

Barber, M. (2012) Promoting Communication rather than Generating Data. In: Hewett, D., (ed.). *Intensive Interaction Theoretical Perspectives,* 1st edn. London, UK: SAGE Publications. pp. 88–103.

Firth, G., Berry, R., and Irvine, C. (2010) *Understanding Intensive Interaction.* London, UK: Jessica Kingsley.

Hewett, D. (2012a) How do Human Beings Start Learning to Communicate. In: Hewett, D., Firth, G., Barber, M. and Harrison, T., (ed.). *The Intensive Interaction Handbook*. London, UK: Sage Publications. pp. 21–25.

Hewett, D. (2012b) Further and Continuing Progress. In: Hewett, D., Firth, G., Barber, M. and Harrison, T., (ed.). *The Intensive Interaction Handbook*. London, UK: SAGE Publications. pp. 21–25.

Hewett, D. (2015) *Intensive Interaction Co-ordinators' Training Course*.

Maslow, A.H. (1943) 'A Theory of Human Motivation.' *Psychological Review* 50(4), pp. 370–396.

Nind, M. and Hewett, D. (2006) *Access to communication: Developing the basics of communication with people with severe learning difficulties through intensive interaction*. 2nd edn. London, UK: David Fulton Publishers.

Chapter 3

Sustaining and developing practice in a large NHS Trust

Jules McKim

Jules gives us an account of his Intensive Interaction journey with Dennis over a period of years. Jules also provides insight into his already established Intensive Interaction Co-ordinator role and the challenge of expanding that role when his Trust (Ridgeway Partnership NHS Trust) was acquired by a much larger NHS Trust (Southern Health NHS Foundation Trust).

Why Intensive Interaction?

Intensive Interaction is

an approach to facilitating two-way communication with people with severe or profound learning disabilities and/or autism, who are still at an early stage of communication development. It can be used to teach people fundamental communication or to provide them with a means to enjoy being expressive and feeling connected. (Dept. of Health, 2009, p.38).

The development, theory and practice of Intensive Interaction is described extensively in books and papers (Nind and Hewett, 1994; Nind and Hewett, 2001; Hewett, 2012; Firth, 2012; and Firth and Barber, 2011). The approach is featured in the Mencap Communication Guidelines (Goldbart and Caton, 2010) and in the Raising Our Sights report (Mansell, 2010). The latter concluded that services have not progressed sufficiently for the benefit of people with more profound learning disabilities and it stated that 'there is great potential here to provide a better quality of life' for such people by using Intensive Interaction (Mansell, 2010, p.13). Following the Raising Our Sights report a series of guides have been produced, several of which specifically recommend Intensive Interaction. Additionally, in 2013, the Royal College of Speech and Language Therapists outlined good communication standards and recommends Intensive Interaction as a valuable and legitimate approach within this framework.

My NHS Trust

I currently work within an NHS Trust across Oxfordshire, Buckinghamshire and Hampshire. Over the past few years, whilst the Learning Disability service has been transferred between different NHS Trusts (Oxfordshire Learning Disability NHS Trust, Ridgeway Partnership NHS Trust, Southern Health NHS Foundation Trust), the service provision has remained essentially the same. We support adults with learning disabilities who have health and social care needs. Our services encompass supporting people in registered care homes, supported living arrangements, day services, respite and outreach services. We also support people within inpatient services. The workforce consists of support staff and managers (within the Social Care Department) and specialist clinicians (as part of the Learning Disability Teams).

Intensive Interaction within my NHS Trust

There has been a long history of staff training, research and development in Intensive Interaction within the Trust, led and championed by Judith Samuel, head of the Psychology Department (McKim, 2013). This dates back to the early 1990s when Melanie Nind, one of the originators of Intensive Interaction (Nind and Hewett, 1994), was working at Oxford Brookes University. She provided some of the initial training to support workers, managers and clinicians.

My role is as the Trust Intensive Interaction Co-ordinator. This position was created following a visit to my Trust by Cath Irvine from the Intensive Interaction Institute in 2007. Cath had trained some of our support staff and managers in Intensive Interaction and this group rolled out the training internally from that point on. With a growing awareness that training alone does not change practice and sustain innovation, Judith Samuel put together a business case for a full-time role. Thus, the Intensive Interaction Co-ordinator role was established, being funded by the Social Care Department, with strong links to the Learning Disability Teams and with line-management and clinical supervision provided by psychologists from within the Psychology Department. In addition to training, support is provided in services through follow-up visits to embed practice and enhance quality.

Within Oxfordshire we support approximately 100 adults with learning disabilities for whom Intensive Interaction is essential. In addition to this on-going development work within our own services, I receive referrals through the Learning Disability Teams across the three counties. These referrals come from family members, other provider organisations and allied healthcare professionals. I provide training directly to the team and wider social network around the individual referred. They are inducted into the theory and practice of Intensive Interaction, being regularly reviewed and given feedback on their progress. Trainees are mostly support staff and managers, but also include family members, advocates and clinicians (doctors, nurses and therapists).

My NHS Trust views the provision of good quality Intensive Interaction as an essential part of the core support for people for whom it is relevant. It is not considered an add-on, or an optional extra. Neither is it something that staff can opt out of if they feel uncomfortable. It has become an expectation of the support worker role. Managers are actively encouraged to monitor the quantity and the quality of the sessions taking place.

Over the last eight years, my team and I have seen many dramatic and positive changes in both the clients' wellbeing, and response to Intensive Interaction and their support workers' attitudes and skills in this field. One manager recently reflected that without Intensive Interaction "the people we support don't have the chance to be people." I feel this reflects my experiences entirely: without direction and encouragement of the staff and the scheduling, supporting and development of their efforts, there is a great risk that the people we support lose their humanity. They become 'processes' with daily 'care' routines, boxes to be ticked. This might mean that their basic physical needs are attended to, but their meaningful communications are limited to 'requests' (asking for food, fluids or toileting) and 'responses' ('high-fives' and other automatic responses). The fun, warmth and richness of human-to-human social engagement is obscured by goal-driven schedules set up for, and managed by, the support workers. And that is not good enough. Intensive Interaction is a low-cost high-impact intervention. It is, simply put, about getting the best out of our staff, and this in turn will allow us to see the best in the people we support.

My team and I continue to raise the profile of Intensive Interaction within our Trust, and this became even more of a priority when we merged with Southern Health NHS Foundation Trust. We wanted both to maintain the support and recognition of what we were already doing, and to look for new opportunities and areas of development.

Further developing my skills in the theory and practice of Intensive Interaction by attending Dave Hewett's Co-ordinator course was essential for professional development and for being able to create a more significant impact across the wider organisation. Working with so many people across a large area, I was looking forward to the contrast of spending focussed quality time with my one case study person and their support staff. It became clear during the course that focussing in this way with one person in one place produces wider benefits in terms of my understanding and ability to influence positive change across the whole area.

When starting the Intensive Interaction Co-ordinator course and thinking about a case study person, I immediately thought of Dennis. He is of a similar age to me and thus I have always felt a sense of connection with him, and been curious about his communication and potential. I feel that in some way we had let him down by starting Intensive Interaction with him in the past but not keeping it going sufficiently. I wondered what had caused the Intensive Interaction to finish. Perhaps it was happening informally and it was the record-keeping and reflection that had finished. Exploring these issues could perhaps ensure that for Dennis, and others, we safeguarded against such 'initiative decay' (Moyes, 2005) reoccurring. The following is an account of his, and my, Intensive Interaction journey.

Dennis

Our first meeting

I first met Dennis in 2005, when I was working as a service manager. Dennis was in the communal room of his shared house. He was lying on the floor, his head underneath a chair, and was busily self-stimulating using rhythmic movements and deep resonant vocalisations. As his housemates had more prominent social behaviours that resulted in their being attended to more frequently, there was a tendency for Dennis to be left to his own devices. He seemed unable to initiate social interactions and therefore meaningful two-way communication was limited.

Dennis had previously received Intensive Interaction, still having the occasional unscheduled session. Staff described his enthusiasm, enjoyment and anticipation for the sessions. He would become very excited when he saw team members who used the approach walking up the garden path. However, due to the other challenges in his environment and the various demands on the staff, Dennis' Intensive Interaction experiences were purely spontaneous; there was little reinforcement or reassurance of regular sessions. More recently, Dennis had appeared to 'refuse' Intensive Interaction. Despite the previous interactions and the good relationships between Dennis and his team of staff, I felt that he remained a 'silent participant' within his home environment, receiving interactions only when it was convenient for the staff (often only when everything else had been done), as opposed to when it was convenient and desirable for him. A lack of guidelines in Dennis' care plan also indicated a lack of prioritisation of the use of Intensive Interaction. Perhaps we could enhance his experiences, satisfaction and confidence through the more focussed use of Intensive Interaction as well as developing recording and reflection. The team took the decision to re-establish a programme of Intensive Interaction with Dennis and improve his communication prospects.

When discussing the above issues with Dennis' support staff, there was a positive response to the 'reintroduction' of Intensive Interaction. There was clearly great warmth for Dennis and a heartening commitment to do all that could be done to improve his quality of life. However, there were a number of comments and issues that rang alarm bells, and which I have since noted in other services where Intensive Interaction is not sufficiently established (see Figure 3.1).

- 'We do Intensive Interaction all the time ...'
- 'We're not very good at filling in forms ...'
- 'The client doesn't want to do Intensive Interaction anymore ...'
- 'We tried it once and he didn't like it ...'
- 'We're communicating with him all the time. I don't see why we have to make it so formal ...'

Figure 3.1 Comments that signify a misunderstanding of Intensive Interaction requirements.

Such comments most likely reflect a misunderstanding of our management expectations, and perhaps of the actual approach itself. Without regular refresher training and in-house mentoring and supervision, I believe Intensive Interaction is poorly understood and poorly practiced. Perhaps these comments also show we have not been clear in our aims. I now needed to demonstrate that it was possible, desirable and useful to plan, schedule, record and reflect on Dennis' sessions, but with an additional emphasis that 'ad hoc' sessions were also welcome. In my experience, the planned sessions tend to go on for longer, to be more meaningful, to be more conversational and reciprocal as opposed to just simple greetings in passing.

An interesting piece of feedback from a number of staff who had tried more formal sessions was "we tried sitting near Dennis and doing Intensive Interaction but he doesn't like it – he pushed us away." I thought that it was crucial to examine this belief in detail and observe what was happening in these situations.

Observations

The first step was to spend time just observing Dennis. As Dave Hewett would say, getting to know the 'Dennisness' of Dennis. What makes him tick? What interests and motivates him? What is he focussing on? What are his eyes and hands doing? What does he do when no-one is asking or directing him to do things? This was done in a structured way and video footage was also taken of Dennis on his own in a number of different settings.

What I noticed is summarised in Figure 3.2.

It felt like there was much that I could try joining in with. It seemed that his positioning was of great importance to him in terms of feeling safe and secure. He seemed interested in people, or perhaps it was more that he was interested in what people could get for him. Staff reported that he could be fun and playful, particularly in the evenings when he would enjoy games of tickling and 'Round and Round the Garden.' With commitments outside of work, I knew it would be difficult to visit Dennis outside of the 9 to 5 Monday to Friday working week. I was also very aware that this might not suit Dennis.

Two years prior to starting the course, I had provided Intensive Interaction training to Dennis' staff team. Some staff had been able to continue and complete reflective accounts of the interactions; others, as described above, felt that Dennis was not interested. When we observed his gesture of 'pushing us away' it became clear that the aim was not always to push staff away. On the contrary, he was trying to redirect staff to stand behind him, to be at the back of his wheelchair: he was asking to go out. What had been interpreted as a negative gesture was, at times, a positive request.

- Fleeting eye contact
- Regular observation of the 'whole space', taking in persons present and ongoing activities
- Rich variety of vocalisations
- Repetitive 'finger–interlocking' gestures using both hands
- Hand clapping
- Right foot to floor thumping
- Right hand to floor slapping
- Right hand to thigh slapping with accompanying backward-glance over the corresponding shoulder
- Tongue 'lick' of the floor or the leg of furniture

Figure 3.2 Dennis' repertoire of communication and self-stimulation.

First interaction – 4th March 2014

Today I lay on the floor facing Dennis, checking quickly that the hoovering had been done. Life carried on around and above us: the other residents and staff walking past and stepping over us. Although I was facing Dennis, I felt that I wasn't too close: at his level and in his field of vision but not 'in his face.' Initially, after saying hello, I just watched and listened. He was very active. Joining in with Dennis' vocalisations is a big step. They are so frequent and so loud that for anyone, joining in is going to well and truly push the button marked 'self-consciousness.'

Initially I began to join in by echoing some of Dennis' vocalisations, as well as the claps and slaps of feet and hands. Very quickly Dennis gave me more eye contact. This continued with repeated glances in my direction. After about five minutes he reached across the floor and took my hand, but then pushed me away. It was a clear signal that he had had enough of my presence. During the interaction, there had been no smiles and I was left wondering if he had enjoyed or merely tolerated my presence. I felt a little awkward at first, especially when on camera. This was such an interesting part of the Co-ordinator Course: the experience of being on film. At first I found myself cringing when watching myself back. Later on in the course it was easier due to familiarity and repetition.

Positioning his head under a chair may provide him with a feeling of safety or it may provide some sort of sensory stimulation, perhaps by amplifying his vocalisations. It is rumoured that he had had his head stomped on in the past, so maybe the protection theory is the closest to the truth of his experience.

A summary of a selection of the sessions based on the notes taken at the time

4th April 2014

Dennis was quite energetic today – lots of movement and vocalisations. It is hard to know what to join in with: doing it all doesn't seem right. I decided to join in with the blowing noises he was making with his mouth, and look for opportunities for engaging in eye contact. Throughout the 20 minutes of doing this, there were frequent smiles from Dennis. I tried joining in with his rocking movements but it didn't seem to generate any interest or curiosity on his part. Dennis frequently looked over his shoulder at his housemates and the staff, but I felt that this reduced when I was sat facing him. I was aware of my agenda in trying to get a good quality film, and how it might be distracting me from being the best interactive partner for Dennis.

There was an unusual ending to this session. Dennis got out of his chair, took my hand and walked through the lounge. He wasn't leading me, it felt like he wanted me to lead him. I wasn't clear where he wanted to go: to his room, to the kitchen or outside the house. I decided to see what would happen if I didn't direct him. We ended up doing a sort of dance around in circles in the lounge, holding hands but going nowhere fast.

24th April 2014

Dennis was quieter, less energetic. I sat quietly with him, waiting. Eye contact began and increased in both frequency and duration during this session. He initiated some interactional behaviours such as clapping. During this session I tried something I hadn't tried before: I 'echoed' Dennis' rocking with sound and movement on the table in front of him. Basically, I scratched the table with my fingernails, in time to his back and forth rocking. He loved this and gave me a big beaming smile as soon as I began doing it. Other observations today were that when C, one of his housemates became louder, Dennis became louder. After 15 minutes Dennis shuffled backwards on his chair, further away from me, but the interaction continued, he seemed to want to stay engaged, but from further away. Turn-taking of clapping increased in these last moments.

1st May 2014

Dennis was vigorously rocking in his chair and repeatedly looking over his shoulder when I arrived. I felt that he was slightly distressed today. There was evidence of recent self-injurious behaviour: red sores on his wrists where he bites himself. This led me into reflecting how, as an infrequent visitor, Dennis didn't have the opportunity to initiate interactions with me *when he wanted to*. This was not ideal as I was no doubt missing opportunities when Dennis was calmer and more sociable. However, this awareness did, if anything, encourage me to be non-directive. I was simply there, available for Dennis to engage with me if he wanted to do so.

A few minutes into this session, Dennis reached across the table and took my hand. I wasn't sure here if he was making social physical contact, trying to move me away or guiding me to take him out. Obvious pleasure from Dennis continued after this, so I could only conclude it was a positive gesture. There seemed to be more continuous smiling from Dennis today. This was corroborated by the member of staff who, on this occasion had been free to hold the camera for me.

15th May 2014

When I arrived Dennis was on the floor in the lounge, the support staff in the kitchen. When I approached him he stood up, took my hand and led me to the kitchen. After a sandwich and drink the session began. Initially I sat on his left but moved to his right-hand side to get better into the shot for the camera. I joined in with clapping, slapping thighs and vocalisations. I also tried varying my responses more than usual and exploring delays and anticipation. The sum total of all this was too much. On reflection later on, I realised I was trying to do too much. I was clearly not content with keeping it simple, and exploring the repertoire we had established. I now understand Dennis needs the familiarity and predictability of repetition – going over old ground and re-exploring our repertoire (Nind and Hewett, 2001).

17th June 2014

Dennis was on the floor so I lay down facing him, joined in with his vocalisations and eye contact. Lots of eye contact today, especially once he became used to the staff member standing near us holding the camera. I tried some very gentle initiations of physical contact but he didn't appear interested.

When I joined-in with a certain movement today – moving his head to the floor while vocalising – he gave me a different quality of eye contact. It was more sustained but also his eyes were full of curiosity.

Again, today felt a little forced. I turned up at 2:00 pm on my timetable, and I wondered how open Dennis was for the interaction. His housemates had been somewhat agitated today and this had stressed Dennis.

7th July 2014

Dennis lying on the floor under a chair again. I lay on the floor facing him and joined in with his vocalisations, responding to him in the spaces between his sounds. C came and sat near us, and was very loud. Dennis seemed to correspondingly increase his vocal volume but seemed quite happy.

Significant today was the amount of smiling and even real laughter, contingent on my responses to him. He signalled more clearly when he had had enough, by turning away.

I now feel that, even if I am rushed as I was today, I can more quickly and easily switch into the right state to do good quality Intensive Interaction. I've always thought that pausing and not doing too much is very difficult if you have a sense of being under pressure. Today I noticed for the first time that whilst I was feeling rushed, I was still able to put it to one side and slow down. I also noticed that today I was louder and clearer with my vocal replies to Dennis. Perhaps this made the difference to his his enjoyment. Previously my vocal replies had been tentative and filled with self-consciousness.

27th August 2014

Dennis on the floor again on my arrival. More self-slapping than usual. Some clapping turn-taking established after a few minutes. I tried frequent touch initiation. On reflection, this was too much. Dennis was less engaged today, with a possible stomach ache, and I was trying hard to 'get him back.' I reported my concerns about his physical health to the staff – his facial expressions seemed to indicate the coming and going of pain.

Around this time, back in Malvern on the next block of the Co-ordinator course, Dave Hewett made a comment that stuck with me. While watching me joining in with many aspects of what Dennis was doing, Dave said it was the vocal echoing, not the clapping, that he was watching. I think I had been too interested in this, over and above the more significant communicative behaviour. Clapping is easier for us to copy than vocalising, it keeps me within my comfort zone. However, the closer I am to my comfort zone, the further I am from Dennis.

8th September 2014

Dennis sat rocking at the dining room table with his back to his housemates and staff. I sat on his right-hand side. After a few moments he leaned forward and pressed his tongue to the table top. This was something new. We took turns doing this (although due to hygiene concerns I didn't use my tongue, but pressed my nose on the surface instead). I waited until he had come back up before I went down so he could see me doing so. Within this I gave him vocal responses too. I think my pausing was better today though, on looking back at the video, I still think I was doing too much, trying too many variations.

Looking back at the video I noticed some significant moments that I had missed at the time:

6:50   Dennis watches me take my turn at licking the table – the first sign that we had true turn-taking, i.e. I wasn't merely filling the gaps in his behaviour … he was giving me gaps to fill, and was interested in the fact that I was filling them with recognisable behaviour.

7:10   Dennis turns to look over his right shoulder – the first time today – and in doing so, gives me a sweep of eye contact.

8:20   His attention goes on for a moment longer than usual, accompanied by a smile.

2nd October 2014

Just after breakfast, drink just finished. Dennis sat at the table, C nearby but quiet. Usual repertoire. Dennis initiated touch three times. The first two occasions seemed to be just for its own sake, the third time was clearly a gesture of pushing me away signalling that he had had enough. I wonder if the movement of reaching out is almost a habit for him.

Dennis has been agitated the last two days. More self-injuring than normal. Night staff reported that he was up and about in his room during the night, looking for his arm-protectors. Learning that he had the ability to problem-solve like this, feeling the urge to self-injure but taking steps to avoid the physical injury, came as a surprise and with it a flood of empathy for the man.

26th November 2014

Today's interaction was significant for its seeming lack of moments of significance. This feeling of normality and doing nothing out of the ordinary was an interesting stage to arrive at. I feel it indicated that I had become genuinely relaxed interacting with Dennis in this way.

We explored similar territory to previously. Taking turns in placing our faces on the table, vocal noises, blowing etc. The house was quiet. At one moment, I think he was perhaps teasing me – he half-leaned to the table top but then came back up smiling. Today he didn't push me away, turn away or otherwise indicate that he had had enough. I finished the session myself after 25 minutes as I had an appointment to go on to. I viewed this absence of a negative (pushing me away) as a positive. I made the following comment on the session sheet:

'Dennis needs lots of interactions like this.'

12th January 2015

Dennis sat at the table. I sat to his left-hand side. He was relatively quiet today but busy: rocking, blowing, clapping, looking over his shoulder. He seemed particularly interested when I joined in with vocalising over my shoulder. At one point, Dennis moved his chair closer to me – I have never noticed that before. Being closer helped – I think. I felt more self-conscious today as there was an agency staff member watching us very closely. As Dennis was giving so much eye contact, I felt a little unsure about how much facial expression I ought to use. How long could I smile for? Could I be overdoing the facial expressions?

20th January 2015

For some reason, I didn't complete a session sheet on this occasion. I felt that it had been a good interaction, I had enjoyed it, and there had been significant eye contact and smiling. Due to an upcoming few days on the Co-ordinator Course, I was gathering my project work together. I realised I needed to reflect on this session, so I sat down to watch the video.

I was closer than normal in my positioning with Dennis. This was due to where he was sitting, where I could balance the camera, and the need to get both of us in the shot. I think this made a significant difference. I can't stress the importance of videoing enough, and this was my personal realisation of this fact. There was so much within this interaction that I had not been aware of at the time. I could see a head-wobbling gesture that I hadn't noticed before, accompanied by a broad grin and sustained eye contact. The word that sprang to mind was 'delight'. Dennis was delighted to see me. Vocalisations were clear, varied and obviously communicative.

27th February 2015

I sat at the table on Dennis' right-hand side; I rocked and moved about in response to him. I also joined in with blowing, puffing and vocalising. It all felt more natural and less forced from my point of view. Today, there were long moments of eye contact, as well as turn-taking of tongue on the table. He moved his chair a little closer three times. Six minutes in he did what I now call a 'happy head scratch' – a wobbling movement of his head along with a rubbing/scratching movement with his right hand across his scalp.

4th March 2015

Sat at the table in the usual place. Dennis was quite animated: puffing and blowing. Delighted head-rubbing at 35 seconds. At three minutes an increase of vocalisations and smiling. At 7:40 I just wrote the word 'happiness'. 8:20 he initiates eye contact and smiles at me. At 11:50 there was a moment of deeper connection, visible on video, very hard to describe in words. He smiled, looked at me and leaned closer, but it was more than that. At 13:20 he leaned forward and touched his tongue to the table, came upright and looked at me as if to say "your turn!"

In total there was less eye contact today, but the moments we exchanged seemed more meaningful, and warmer. Much of the time he seemed to be interested in watching my hands, which were joining in with some of his complex patterns of finger movements.

We were both a little distracted today as an inevitable result of doing the sessions out in a communal area, as opposed to in Dennis' room or in a sensory room. I feel strongly that it is best to meet the person you are going to interact with where they are. If we move someone to a quieter room, we have immediately taken control. Dennis likes to be in this open area with people to watch. Although the other people may distract us from each other, they can provide a joint focus. Sitting quietly in a room on our own may have been too much.

Another aspect of performing publicly was that other people could see the interactions. I viewed this as having immense benefits. Firstly, by having no sense of hidden practice or mystery. Secondly, to demonstrate how to do Intensive Interaction with Dennis. And thirdly, to work toward normalising it.

Feedback from other trainee Co-ordinators

I felt this to be the most valuable, rewarding and insightful aspect of the course. The perception, insight and creativity of my colleagues on this course never ceased to amaze me. Viewing videos together with peers and colleagues is an invaluable addition to reflective practice, and essential for training and developing staff. The Coordinator Course is divided into blocks of three days and starting on Block 2 a video feedback protocol is used to develop practice. Good aspects of technique (positive/technical) are described explicitly and accurately; suggestions for improvement or development (constructive/reflective) are offered in the form of open questions to the practitioner. The positive/technical feedback gave us each a list of things we were doing right. The constructive/reflective feedback opened up our thinking and gave suggestions, ideas, views from a different perspective to take back to the interactions next time. These sessions were extremely valuable: always a bit challenging, always thoroughly rewarding.

Positive/technical feedback from Block 2:

- Good positioning in his eye-line
- Use of changes and 'different' responses deepened his interest in you
- Good pausing – you let him lead and be in control
- It was obvious that you were both having fun
- The use of physical contact fitted in well with the flow of the interaction
- I liked how you started slow and held back, gathered momentum/tempo and increased proximity at the same time

Constructive/reflective feedback from Block 2

- At the beginning Dennis was wiggling his toes. Had you thought of ways to respond to this?
- What made you know when to touch him?
- Regarding positioning – do you feel he needs a particular amount of space between you?
- The 'game' of reaching out and initiating physical contact – does he do this at other times/in other situations?
- Could you do more within the realm of physical contact? What would that look like?

Mentoring staff

During the latter stages of the case-study work, we were required to mentor one member of staff in the service. I had two willing participants: Theresa and Kat. They stood out from within the staff team, as they were both enthusiastic and had no concerns about being filmed.

What was immediately surprising to me was that when put on the spot, they did not do Intensive Interaction. Their interactions were kind and well-meaning, but very directive and not very tuned in to Dennis. They had both attended the one-day training I deliver within the Trust. This highlighted the major issue that classroom style training does not change people's practice. This experience of mentoring was so important in developing my understanding of supporting behaviour change, that I now ensure I include it within all clinical interventions.

Theresa was highly directive, talking continuously to Dennis, tickling him, trying to get him to engage. Part of this was clearly the pressure of being filmed. It took careful discussions to adjust her style to one of still being engaged and tuned-in: not doing, but rather waiting and responding. As support workers – I include myself in here – we are just not used to doing this. We have built a career on prompting, directing, correcting, controlling, guiding people 'hand-over-hand.' Soon enough though, Theresa became rather wonderful. Her humour and playfulness was intact and Dennis began to spark off that.

Kat was also self-conscious being filmed. During her initial interaction she was clearly not relaxed, and seemed rather detached and distant. She would occasionally reach forward and touch Dennis' foot and vocalise, using his sounds, but not in response to him. Although not as directive as Theresa initially, she was not responsive. Once again, with sensitive discussions including identifying and praising the positives along with honest and explicit constructive feedback, Kat was able to quieten, soften, and tune-in to Dennis.

The single most effective technique for developing staff skills in this area is the use of video. My work with my mentees mirrored that of the Co-ordinator Course itself. A videoed interaction would be watched together, and I would offer positive and technical comments followed by constructive and reflective feedback. In practice, however, both Theresa and Kat would be quite self-critical and could clearly see where they lost the purity of the approach. My role here was then one of reassurance, affirmation, and highlighting the details of what they did well.

Outcomes – for Dennis and myself

Outcomes for myself were rich, varied and somewhat unexpected. These are summarised in Figure 3.3 below:

Outcomes for Dennis are indicated in the following comments:

- 'In my opinion Dennis has become quite social. So much so that when the builders were in making a real racket, Dennis sat in his chair right in the doorway watching what was going on. Previously he would have been disturbed by having strangers in his house.' Emma, Care Service Co-ordinator
- 'I was amazed at the level of engagement.' Ivana, Care Service Co-ordinator
- Increased eye contacts and smiling during interactions in general. 'Everyone's noticed the change in Dennis.' Theresa, Support Worker
- He no longer 'ends' sessions by pushing partner away.
- He is spending much less time lying on the floor. It's as if he is consciously positioning himself where he can engage with people more easily.

Organisational development

Perhaps the most significant act I facilitated was inviting my Chief Executive to visit one of the Supported Living services in Oxfordshire. I chose one of the homes where the staff

---

- I got to know Dennis – as a person, not as a client with labels and a medical history, but as a person in the here and now with a rich communicative repertoire and a cheeky sense of humour.
- Working so closely with one person for a year put me up against issues of wanting progress, which I often hear from a lot of staff. Hence, it helped me to better empathise with staff, and be more effective at communicating within and around this topic during training and mentoring.
- I can switch from being busy and in a rush, to being quietly and mindfully focussed much quicker than I previously could.
- I have developed the language of giving warm, supportive feedback – both positive and filled with praise and constructive/corrective.
- I have become a better practitioner of Intensive Interaction: more able to tune in, pause and be responsive.

Figure 3.3 Personal outcomes as a result of this focussed work with Dennis.

practiced Intensive Interaction at a good level. To some extent the staff here are 'naturals.' Our Chief Executive was very impressed by the quality of the interactions that she observed, and, as planned, it helped raise the profile of the approach within the Trust. I was invited to present at the Trust Board and invited to provide training to other services, including a dementia ward in older people's mental health services.

I've always tried to maintain a visible profile within my organisation, at all levels. Whenever presenting to the senior management team, I will always show a video of an interaction of someone who uses our services locally, and who the managers present know. Over the duration of the course, I pledged to extend this 'visibility campaign' into the new Trust we had merged with. This involved writing articles to include in the *Southern Health Journal*, having a stand at staff away days, presenting to managers at any and every opportunity, as well as developing an on-line presence within the staff intranet and the public website.

Having time away from the 'coal face' of clinical responsibilities during the Co-ordinator course has allowed more strategic planning. To this end, I developed a three-year strategic plan and a SWOT (Strengths-Weaknesses-Opportunities-Threats) analysis that were presented to the senior management team. As the clinical framework of interventions via the Learning Disability Teams was being developed at this time, I ensured that Intensive Interaction was included as a possible intervention within several of the CAPs (Clinical Areas of Practice) and specified in the pathway documents: *Autism, Complex Health, Challenging Behaviour* and *Dementia*.

Promoting Intensive Interaction as a clear, practical technique to develop rapport has been a useful way to frame the approach to fit into Positive Behavioural Support plans. This has been an effective way to get involved in improving people's quality of life when in community settings, so as to avoid hospital admissions due to behavioural issues. Several referrals have come in via the Intensive Support Teams as a result of this promotional work.

Integration and partnership working is a big agenda item within the NHS. Intensive Interaction seemingly has a wide application: children and adult services, learning disabilities, mental health, and older people's services. So, making connections, doing presentations and forging plans for pilot projects has all blossomed out of this work.

Towards the end of the Co-ordinator course, we spent time discussing organisational change and specifically Lewin's theories of force field analysis (Lewin, 1951). I had an in-depth discussion with a colleague on the course and identified both:

Driving forces:

- Supportive management
- National recommendation of Intensive Interaction
- It is person-centred, person-led, secures choice and control
- The videos speak for themselves!
- We are giving a voice to the 'voiceless'

Restraining forces:

- Some staff attitudes
- Staff turnover
- Care Quality Commission (CQC) knowledge and expectations
- Distance between managers and people we support

- The tricky issue of outcome measurements
- It may not look like you are working when you are doing Intensive Interaction

By overcoming weak restraining forces, quick gains may lead easily to observable outcomes and changes. Moderate and strong restraining forces may need 'unfreezing' before change can happen. Reducing the weak restraining forces will weaken the moderate and strong forces (Lewin, 1951). This theoretical framework, discussion and reflection led me to make an ultimate action plan, which will probably still be pinned to my office notice board on the day I retire.

'To do list' or future recommendations

- Develop an organisational Intensive Interaction webpage: include the Fundamentals of Communication (Nind and Hewett, 2001 – see appendix 1), rolling photos, short video clips.
- Develop display boards in key locations across the geographical area.
- Get really good at video editing.
- Put all useful documents on the shared drive so all managers can access.
- Ensure that Intensive Interaction is specified within people's care plans as an essential component of their support.
- Produce person-centred communication DVDs for every person we support. A video of how that person communicates will be vastly superior to a file full of forms and written guidelines.
- Identify and work with an Intensive Interaction champion in each service. Champions to be the lead person in supporting the provision of sessions and completion of session forms. They will be a point of contact for myself and the senior managers.
- Ensure there is a management expectation in place regarding the provision of Intensive Interaction sessions and associated evidence of reflection.
- Stay up-to-date with all national and organisational policies, acts, drives and changes, and ensure what I promote fits with the current vernacular.
- Engage more with commissioners and care managers to promote the approach, to share expectations of services once I have made recommendations to a service or team.
- Modify job descriptions to include the 'provision of meaningful two-way communication.'
- Trial a variety of outcome measurement tools, and use one which works best.
- Influence the recruitment process – develop more value-based recruitment. Personalise this further for the staff who support people for whom Intensive Interaction is relevant.
- Develop supportive guidance and policies, especially touch guidance.
- Influence local audit and inspection frameworks to ensure they include assessment of Intensive Interaction provision.

Some of these points have been achieved. Some are ongoing. Some are in the realm of 'north star dreams' to guide progress and direction: completing them is perhaps not the point (O'Brien, Pearpoint and Kahn, 2010). We all have to aim high. We also need to be realistic and celebrate the small steps we have taken, and acknowledge the people whose lives have changed as a result of this wonderful approach.

Dennis continues to enjoy being expressive and has regular opportunities to feel connected. Committing to and scheduling the use of Intensive Interaction ensures it will continue. Developing guidelines for inclusion in his care plan will help to ensure that the provision of good quality Intensive Interaction remains a central part of his life, all his life.

Acknowledgements

Many thanks to Samantha Chudleigh-Warren for helping with editing, making this chapter more readable, and her on-going enthusiasm for Intensive Interaction.

References

Department of Health. (2009) Valuing People Now: a new three-year strategy for people with learning disabilities. HMSO, London.

Firth, G. and Barber, M. (2011) *Using Intensive Interaction with a person with a social or communicative impairment.* London, UK: Jessica Kingsley Publishers.

Firth, D. (2012) Background to Intensive Interaction. In: Hewett, D., Firth, G., Barber, D., Harrison, T., (ed.). *The Intensive Interaction Handbook.* London, UK: SAGE Publications. pp. 9–20.

Goldbart, J. and Catons, S. (2010) *Communication and People with the Most Complex Needs: What Works and Why This is Essential. Mencap.* London, UK.

Hewett, D. (2012) What is Intensive Interaction? Curriculum, Process, and Approach. In: Hewett, D, (ed.). *Intensive Interaction. Theoretical Perspectives.* SAGE Publications: London, UK. pp. 137–154.

Lewin, K. (1951) *Field Theory in Social Science.* New York, NY: Harper and Row.

Mansell, J. (2010) *Raising our Sights: Services for Adults with Profound Intellectual and Multiple Disabilities.* London, UK: Department of Health (see also Government response on DoH website).

McKim, J. (2013) 'Developing the use of Intensive Interaction in the Oxfordshire Learning Disability NHS Trust' (Ridgeway Partnership). *Clinical Psychology and People with Learning Disabilities,* 11(1&2) pp. 12–19.

Moyes, T. (2005) Presentation on Identifying 'Initiative Decay,' and reducing its effects. *UK Intensive Interaction Conference.* Leeds, UK: Leeds Mental Health NHS Trust.

Nind, M. and Hewett, D. (1994) *Access to Communication: Developing the Basics of Communication with People with Severe Learning Disabilities Through Intensive Interaction.* London, UK: David Fulton.

Nind, M. and Hewett, D. (2001) *A Practical Guide to Intensive Interaction.* Kidderminster, UK: British Institute of Learning Disabilities.

O'Brien, J., Pearpoint, J. and Kahn, L. (2010) *The PATH and MAPS Handbook: Person-Centred Ways to Build Community.* Toronto, Canada: Inclusion Press.

Royal College of Speech and Language Therapists. Five good communication standards. London, UK: RCSLT, 2013.

Chapter 4

Learning together through human connection

Individualised care at its best

Michelle Murphy

Michelle writes from the point of view of a learning disability nurse working in a typical service in the Republic of Ireland. She relates her journey with John, who blossomed through the use of Intensive Interaction. Michelle talks with great enthusiasm about the simplicity of Intensive Interaction and the crucial impact it has on communication and well being. She also makes reference to attachment theory and Maslow's hierarchy of needs in order to promote the role of social interactions within the provision of adult residential services.

John and Intensive Interaction

John is a 37-year-old man residing in a house supporting adults with severe and profound intellectual disabilities. John has a loving family who regularly visit. John is a fun-loving man who is a loyal friend to his peers and has been observed to advocate on their behalf, for example if a peer drops a toy they are playing with, John will vocalise loudly to alert staff and stop once his peer has been supported. On rare occasions, John will go and pick the toy up for them and place it on their activity table top. John enjoys being surrounded by social activity. However, John will remain a passive observer unless supported to actively engage.

John frequently rocks backwards and forwards and swings a sock in his hand. Sitting with John and joining in with these movements, that are so familiar and reassuring to him, provided an initial break-through in terms of engaging with him. John has a variety of interesting facial expressions and vocal sounds. Although he does not speak, he uses these expressions and vocalisations to communicate his needs and choices. In order to truly connect with John, we work in partnership with him, and adapt our style of communication to suit his, in an attempt to learn his language. By observing his communicative expressions closely, we gain significant insight into what John is saying through using them. We sit with John, for no other reason than to connect with him. We pay uninterrupted attention to his intrinsic communicative means, tuning in to his varied facial expressions, wide range of vocalisations, repetitive body movements, expressive gestures and body language. We are beginning to join John in his world and try to see the world as he experiences it. We consciously respect and validate John's unique communicative style by responding; joining in with the things he can understand and by remaining focussed, engaged and present. John has full control of these interactions and we follow his lead at his pace. We realise the importance of dropping our own agenda or any objectives we may have and slowing our pace in order to connect with John. In doing this, we are giving John a framework to support and enable him to connect with us. This is Intensive Interaction.

Communication – reflecting on current practice

The past two decades have seen dramatic improvements in service provision in Ireland with an emphasis on supporting and enabling people with intellectual disabilities to live their lives to the fullest. There is an increased focus on enhancing quality of life through person-centred support, and enhancing social participation and experience. However, providing this support for people with severe and profound intellectual disabilities can be challenging due to the severity of communication difficulties and complexity of communication needs. Communication is an essential requirement of social participation and the establishment of close interpersonal relationships. It is an essential component in supporting social and emotional well being.

As a Registered Nurse in Intellectual Disability (RNID), I am acutely aware of my professional and moral responsibilities to provide support from an emotional, social and communicative perspective.

Health Information and Quality Authority (HIQA, 2013) has identified supporting communication as a basic service registration requirement, and an essential skill in facilitating participation, choice and advocacy (Table 4.1).

In attempting to meet the communication needs of those I support, prior to using Intensive Interaction, my efforts were often directive and functional. I was supporting people in being present at activities (such as walks outside, music sessions, movies) and felt I was supporting people to engage in social interaction by doing this. Why then was I left feeling so inadequate? One day I had been out walking with John who although mobile, requires use of a wheelchair during longer walks. On return from our walk, I documented our 'social' activity in John's support plan. On reflection, I began to think about how much *actual human interaction and connection* John had experienced during this activity. I realised that John had sat facing away from me and couldn't even see my face. I had missed a valuable opportunity to support John to engage and participate, for social interaction and human connection. I began to observe many missed opportunities for human connection and social interaction. On paper, John was attending lots of social activities. However, the *actual level of participation* and *active engagement* from John was minimal and often non-existent.

1: Residents rights, dignity and consultation
Residents are consulted with and participate in decisions about their care.
Residents are enabled to exercise choice and control over their lives in accordance with their preferences.
The complaints of each resident, family member, advocate are listened to.

2: Communication
Residents are able to communicate at all times.
Effective and supportive interventions are provided to residents to ensure their communication needs are met.

3: Family, personal relationships and links within the community
Residents are supported to develop and maintain personal relationships and links with the wider community.

4: Social care needs
Each resident has opportunities to participate in meaningful activities.
Personal plans are drawn up with the maximum participation of each resident.

Table 4.1 Adapted from the registration outcomes of the National Standards for Residential Services for Children and Adults with Disabilities, HIQA (2013).

John enjoys these activities, and they meet his expressed desire to be near social groups. During these activities, however, people with severe/profound intellectual disabilities and complex communication needs are often spectators rather than *active* participants. This type of activity alone is insufficient in promoting the spontaneous, natural and meaningful interactions that are central to human experience.

It is easy for me to attribute this to staffing levels and busy daily routines. However, valuable opportunities to support social interaction were constantly presenting themselves and yet I was not capitalising on them. I have spent considerable time reflecting on this and have identified two main influencing factors:

1   Due to the severity and complexity of their communication needs, the people I support could not verbally request my interaction and attention.
2   Due to my limited education on communication approaches which facilitate social inter-action for people with severe and complex communication needs, I did not have the necessary skills and knowledge to support and maximise social interactions with them.

I needed a communication approach that could enhance *my own* communication skills so that I, in turn could support the communication needs of the people I was supporting. We needed an approach that could facilitate us supporting each other in developing our communication skills together and enable us to engage and connect.

Augmentative Alternative Communication (AAC) systems can be inappropriate for people with severe/profound intellectual disability. These approaches are incompatible with the developmental and functioning ability of people with such levels of intellectual ability. There is also a tendency for support interventions to focus on functional aspects of communication.

Human communication can be social and functional by nature. Maslow (1943) describes functional communication as a type of communication that people use to get their *basic needs* met, such as food, water, sleep, etc. However, supporting functional communication does little to foster relationships and social interactivity. According to Firth, Berry and Irvine (2010, p. 77):

> these systems, and functional communication itself, do not lend themselves to a sustained and sociable two-way conversation. Once a functional need is communicated and successfully responded to, then the reason to communicate is exhausted.

If our sole focus is on supporting functional communication, we cannot address and support a person's need for social interaction and human connection. Yet functional communication is often prioritised over social interaction. Take a moment and imagine what life would be like if we just spoke to each other in order to have our functional needs met ('*What time is the next bus?,*' '*Can I have the roast chicken please?*'). Our social world would be quite empty and under-stimulating. I can't imagine a life without engaging in regular chit-chat. Everyday non-functional conversations serve a very important function. It is these 'non-functional' exchanges that provide us with the social interaction that stimulates our interests, facilitates expression of our individuality, and fosters therapeutic relationships which enhance our emotional well-being. There is a scarcity of communication interventions that support people with severe/profound intellectual disability to experience this two-way, meaningful, conversational com-munication. I needed to identify a communication approach that adequately facilitated this. My search led me to the Intensive Interaction Institute.

Observing through an unhurried lens

I was supported to attend and complete my training as an Intensive Interaction Co-ordinator in 2015 and to pilot the use of Intensive Interaction with one of the people I support.

John would sit in the most social area of the house, and was an interested spectator of social activity. I had a strong feeling John wanted to socially connect and by using Intensive Interaction with John, maybe I could learn how to speak his language and reach him. With the support of John's family, my Clinical Nurse Manager (CNM2) and the Speech and Language Therapy (SLT) Department, we began pre-Intensive Interaction observations with John. Data collection was based on objective and subjective observations and gathered over a two-week period, by both the SLT and me. Supporting John for 12 hours a day provided me with the opportunity to observe and video record John's behaviours for 15 minute periods at varied times each day. Pre-arranged observation times were agreed with the SLT. By pausing to observe John for short intervals during the day, we were able to see him from a very different perspective. His intrinsically unique and varied expressions, vocalisations, body language and patterns of behaviour were now seen through an unhurried lens. We were rewarded with observational data which provided us with an insightful perspective of John's world.

Intensive Interaction – your objective is to drop your own agenda/objective.

> When we focus on ourselves, our world contracts and preoccupations loom. But when we focus on others, our world expands and we increase our capacity for connection. (Goleman, 2004)

The objective with Intensive Interaction is to enter an interaction with John with no other objective than to just be with him. As a healthcare professional, I realise the importance of documentation. Within services there is a justifiable need to provide documentation which reflects support. This is provided by means of individualised goals, the action plan detailing supports required to achieve these goals and evidence to support attainment. Therefore, action plans are often SMART (Specific, Measurable, Achievable, Realistic, Time-framed), placing emphasis on achieving measurable outcomes within a specific time frame. I fear however, that over emphasis on SMART objectives can lead to support becoming task orientated, with objectives attached to every area of support.

When we look at the area of human interaction, SMART targets do not apply. This type of action plan may work well when teaching certain *functional* tasks, that require being broken down into measurable, obtainable steps. However, the sheer complexity of human interaction makes it impossible to be broken down into SMART objectives. In our everyday lives, we do not objectify our chit-chat and interactions. It is a natural, spontaneous process. Whilst not disputing the justified need for setting individualised objectives and documenting attainments, I feel there is an over-emphasis on providing support that can be objectified and documented. This creates the potential to make residential environs so far removed from the natural interactive experiences within most of our homes, that they are in danger of becoming task- rather than person-orientated. Over emphasis on setting and satisfying objectives may restrict people with complex communication needs from experiencing the responsive, free-flowing and socially motivating environment that is so fundamental to facilitating social human connection.

Why is it so essential that we drop our own objective?

Learning to communicate and interact is a complex process. It cannot be broken down into linear form. Most of this learning takes place before we are two years old. The learning that takes place through our earliest interactions is very sophisticated. It is reciprocal. We are processing information at very high speeds. We cannot process it consciously. We learn by unconsciously 'reading' the wide varieties of facial expressions, body language and verbal tones we are receiving in our interactions with others. Then we unconsciously process them. We respond with our own wide and varied facial expressions, body language and verbal tones. We learn the skills necessary to communicate with other people by *actively engaging in this communication process*. This process is repeated and practised over and over again. It is natural and because it is unconscious, we do not have to think about how we first learned to communicate and interact. Intensive Interaction aims to recreate this natural human interactive process for people whose communication skills are still at this early developmental stage. It can therefore be understood as an active learning scenario, where it is essential that the person we are supporting is *actively participating*. The learning can only take place through active participation. When participating in Intensive Interaction, it is vital that John decides the particular focus, method and pace of learning. His engagement in the process needs to be as a result of his own internal motivation (Firth et al., 2010). If we begin to try to apply our own objectives, we catastrophically interrupt the natural engagement and internal motivation that is so essential for John's learning to take place.

> 'A central principle in Intensive Interaction is that communication is a dynamic process which cannot be divided into its component parts for teaching, but must be supported within fluid and learner-led sequences of action learning' (Barber, 2012, p. 95)

The content of our interactions with John needs to follow his focus rather than any agenda we may have. This ensures interactions are intrinsically motivating to John. We cannot limit our responses in favour of those that may seem conventionally appropriate. We need to support John in exploring the possibilities of interactive response, by responding in a way that is meaningful to him. Success of the interaction is not dependant on John's interactive skills, but rather on our ability as his skilled communication partners to interpret and respond to any behaviour John demonstrates, in a manner which intrigues him and invites his continued involvement. As an RNID working frontline, I began to capitalise on all opportunities to connect with John through Intensive Interaction. Following the observational period, I began to build Intensive Interaction into all my interactions with John. I encouraged my colleagues to do the same and they did.

> I come and sit at John's right side and join in his hand movements, raspberry blowing, vocalisations. I respond in every way I can to what he does, in a way I feel he will understand. I keep my facial expressions interested and available and display my genuine interest in keeping him company. He is very interested in what I am doing. Eye contact is becoming more prolonged. John relaxes significantly and all self-stimulating behaviour stops as he becomes more interested in me being there. John reaches out his left hand and grasps my finger and keeps it held in his grasp. This is the first time I have seen John initiate contact. (Staff nurse)

Slow the pace and connect

We can often communicate with the people we support in ways that are far too complex and sophisticated for them to understand and keep up with. The time it takes for people with severe and profound learning disabilities to process the information they are receiving, plan a response and implement it, is often far slower than we anticipate and indeed accommodate. In order to fully relate to each person we support in a respectful manner, we need to adapt the pace of our interactions to meet the pace of the individual. In effect, we need to slow down. The use of any approach to develop a person's communication skills depends on every day natural opportunities for communication. Early communication skills are learnt in this way and not by being 'taught' in sessions. Similarly, a person who is at an early stage of communication needs to be supported to develop their skills in this way. We need to slow our pace and prioritise social interaction to capitalise on all available opportunities to interact and connect.

Intensive Interaction and fostering relationships

Initially as I sat with John on the couch swinging a sock, I was conscious that my colleagues might think I was doing nothing! In fact, as the weeks went on, they became very interested in what I was doing and why. What I was doing was arguably the most important intervention for John.

There is little focus on fostering therapeutic relationships between staff and those they support in residential settings, often due to the misconception that spending quality time actively supporting social interaction is less important than other goal orientated tasks. I feel it is necessary to emphasise the importance of supporting communication, of honouring each person's abilities and of fostering therapeutic relationships. In order to do this I needed to adopt and refer to a humanistic school of thought (Maslow, 1943). The positive effects therapeutic relationships can have on our social and emotional wellbeing, mental health and ultimately our quality of life cannot be underestimated. Firth et al. (2010) believe that a positive attachment relationship is critical for emotional and social development, enabling us to develop a positive view of ourselves.

Attachment is the term given to a special emotional relationship that involves an exchange of comfort, care, and pleasure. John Bowlby (1988, p. 120) believed that *'we are born ready to make attachments because these relationships keep us close to our caregivers and so keep us safe from harm'*.

Bowlby (1969, p. 194) describes attachment as a *'lasting psychological connectedness between human beings.'* He believed our early experiences in childhood influence our development and behaviour later in life. Our early attachment styles are established in childhood through the relationship we have with our caregiver.

From discussions with John's family it is clear that John has developed close attachments with his parents and siblings. Psychology reports of John at three years old observe John to be 'kissing the baby in the mirror'. He was also observed to respond well to his sister's attention, and to vocalise words such as 'mama' and 'dada'.

'*The propensity to make strong emotional bonds to particular individuals [is] a basic component of human nature*' (Bowlby, 1988, p. 3). Most of us have someone in our lives with whom we have established positive attachment, someone we go to for comfort and reassurance. Someone we feel safe with, someone who accepts us for who we are and provides us with a feeling of love and belonging. We have someone who looks forward to seeing us, spending time with us, and who misses us when we are not there. Bowlby (1988) identified four distinguishing characteristics of attachment. I am interested in these characteristics in relation to gaining a better understanding of the social and emotional needs of the people I support and in evaluating how we can enable them to experience these positive human attachments.

1 **Proximity Maintenance** – The desire to be near the people we are attached to.
2 **Safe Haven** – Returning to the attachment figure for comfort and safety in the face of a fear or threat.
3 **Secure Base** – The attachment figure acts as a base of security from which the child can explore the surrounding environment.
4 **Separation Distress** – Anxiety that occurs in the absence of the attachment figure.

John lived at home during his childhood, attending the residential house in which he now lives for occasional respite stays. John has been living in this house full time for many years now. I expect it was very difficult for John to adapt to living without the presence of his family and attachment figures. John's family are supportive of him and visit regularly. John expresses discomfort with, and is upset by change, which causes me to speculate that the move to full time residence had a significant effect on John. It is difficult for John to establish new attachment relationships when there are so many different people supporting him. I believe Intensive Interaction can foster positive therapeutic relationships between John and those supporting him.

Two months after beginning Intensive Interaction with John, I received an insightful email from John's brother …

> *I have noticed the positive changes in John the last day and his more open and outward looking demeanour, as has my sister. He seems to be more responsive and is starting to interact a little more with the world around him. He would have been a little like that a number of years ago, but seemed to have lost it somewhere along the line and started to really go into himself. I think you are getting him to come out of himself again which is fantastic – I think he is really enjoying this which is making us happy.*

This email prompted me to further question why we were finding it so difficult to connect with John. Was our inability to connect with John attributed to the severity of his intellectual disability (as is so often assumed)? Is there a reasonable possibility that it is us, the people supporting John who lack the communication skills needed to develop his ability and desire to communicate and connect?

In 'A theory of human motivation' (1943), Abraham Maslow proposes that human needs have a predetermined order of importance (Figure 4.1).

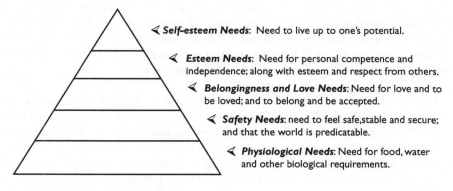

Figure 4.1 Maslow's Hierarchy of Needs.

This pyramid portrays these needs in order of importance and the pyramid reads from the bottom to the top. Maslow's theory assumes that if a person's needs are not met at the lower levels, then they are unable to attend to their needs at higher levels. For a person to attend to higher level needs, deficits at lower levels must be satisfied (Firth, Berry and Irvine, 2010). If we accept Maslow's theory, we can consider that for John to establish a sense of love and belonging, his basic need for a sense of security must be met. Subsequently, for John to establish self-esteem, any deficits in his sense of love and belonging need to be addressed and satisfied. It is my experience that residential settings can find it challenging to meet peoples' need for a sense of security, love and belonging and self-esteem due to difficulty in establishing close relationships. I feel this is especially so for people with severe and profound learning disabilities and complex communication needs.

Carl Rogers (1957) believed that the creation of a growth-producing climate in a therapeutic relationship is characterised by three core conditions.

— **Be genuine or congruent** – in which the carer conveys the message that it is not only permissible but desirable to be oneself.
— **Offer unconditional positive regard and total acceptance**. Occurs when the carer is able to embrace this attitude of acceptance and non-judgement.
— **Feel and communicate a deep empathic meaning**. When this is present the carer demonstrates a capacity to track and sense accurately the feelings and personal meanings of the person and communicate to the person this sensitive and empathic understanding.

'Empathic understanding restores to the lonely and alienated individual a sense of belonging to the human race' (Rogers, 1957).

To be understood in this way can, for many people with severe learning disabilities, be a rare and even unique experience. It indicates to them preparedness on the part of the person supporting them to offer attention and a level of caring which undeniably endows them with value. These core conditions are intrinsic to Intensive Interaction – which involves the person supporting John attuning to his mood, preferences, tempo, and emotional state.

Fostering attunement is a core aspect of Intensive Interaction and an essential component of emotional development. If we are accurately attuned to another person, we are accurately sharing something of what they are experiencing. Attunement involves a certain type of imitation but is not an exact copy of what a person does. Exact copying of what a person does would gain and maintain attention only on the *external* behaviours of the person. Attunement is a different type of imitation. It is about reflecting some understanding of what is going on inside. Matching involves a different mode than the original. What is being matched is some aspect of the behaviour that seems to match the person's *feeling state*. Reflecting back feeling states during interactions with John is important in supporting him to acknowledge his own affectivity on others and develop his sense of self. (Stern, 2000)

> *Five months after beginning to use Intensive Interaction with John, during an II session he became sad, vocalising his sadness in an expressive tone and facial mannerisms, and holding eye contact in shared connectivity. I could really sense his sadness and validated this in the tone of my own responses. I reached out and put my hand on his foot. As soon as I touched him it was as though he sensed my empathy, my acceptance and some of my warmth reassured him and his tension released. He pulled me into hug him, and began sobbing on my shoulder. This is the first time I had seen John cry. (*staff nurse*)*

Daniel Stern (2000) studied the interpersonal world of the infant and identified a series of stages of interpersonal development. I am interested in this as many of the people I support are at these very early stages of development. Having an awareness of these stages will enhance my ability to create and provide experiences that will support their individual developmental needs.

Stern's four interrelated senses of self (Stern, 2000).
- **Emergent Self (0-2 months)** – The infant experiences the world through unrelated sensory stimuli, which they gradually learn how to put together.
- **Core Self (2–7 months)** – The infant is now beginning to be able to organise the sensory experience to have integrated memories. The infant develops a higher level of sophistication (or *emotional intelligence*). They are developing the ability to discern objectives from all the sensory stimuli they are receiving, put this information together and use it to make assumptions as to what they can expect from their environment. It is at this stage that the infant begins to learn what type of behaviours and responses he can expect from their caregiver in specific situations. Many people with severe and profound learning disabilities are at this stage of emotional development. Being aware of this enables me to adapt my responses to John in a way that he can understand and which validates his communicative efforts, in the hope that this instils him with an expectation of positive response.
- **Subjective Self (7–15 months)** – The child begins to realise that there is a gap between his/her subjective reality and other peoples', that they have a mind and feelings and other people have a mind and feelings too. Through attunement with their primary caregiver, the child learns how to bridge this gap through sharing their focus of attention.
- **Verbal Self (15 months onwards)** – Symbolic representation and language acquisition.

These stages are a natural developmental process. It is extremely complex learning, obtained in a very natural, simplistic way. As with Bowlby, Fry and Ainsworth (1990), Stern (2000) sees interpersonal relationships as vital for the development of the various senses of self and believes that disturbances to the development of these stages can have a damaging effect on a person's social and emotional development.

> *John was sitting in the hall, throwing his sock. He was laughing and vocalising when a staff member was picking it up and giving it back to him. As this sequence was repeated, he began to anticipate interaction with staff. At one stage, a staff nurse and two peers were standing near John. John went over and sat in the middle of them, smiling and making eye contact. They responded positively with running commentary. Then he went back to the couch, laughing. I have never seen him do this before.* (support worker)

> *John was standing by the door of the music room, unable to open it. He looked around and walked towards me, took my hand in his and led me to the door. I opened it for him. This is the first time I have been approached by John and the first time I had seen him use gestural prompting and advocate his needs.* (staff nurse)

Learning together

What we learned from John

We learned so much from John. He showed us that it was us, the people supporting him, who did not possess the communication skills necessary to connect with him and not the other way around. He showed us the importance of adapting our style of communication to suit his, and by doing so he could help us to learn how to speak his language. He taught us that there are multiple and varied ways of communicating, and he shared his most creative ways with us. He taught us that if we paid enough attention he would be able to show us how to interpret these creative expressions. He demonstrated that he always had the ability to advocate on behalf of himself and to make choices. It was us who needed to develop the communication skills necessary to support him and interpret what he was trying to say. He helped us to realise that the more connected we were to the people we support, the more fulfilling our role became.

He taught us the importance of being present and engaged; apart from his family, we were the most influential people in his life. He made us realise the direct effect our positive or negative interactions had on his wellbeing and development. He highlighted the dramatic influence a person's social and interactive environment can have on their actual ability and desire to communicate. John is an amazing young man and I am very grateful to him for his participation and for all that he has taught us.

What John learned from us

Written recording sheets and video clips covering a time-period prior to the commencement of the programme, immediately after the programme began and several months into the programme, were evaluated by the multi-disciplinary team. These team members consisted of John's SLT, the Senior Clinical Psychologist, the Clinical Nurse Specialist (Positive Behavioural Support) and myself (RNID).

The following observations were made:

- Vast improvements in areas of spontaneous interaction were observed, with an increase in John's levels of interaction and in his periods of content behaviour.
- John began to respond when people called his name, by looking in their direction.
- John showed greater ability to focus and attend to external stimuli.
- John appeared to make and maintain eye contact with staff and peers for longer periods of time. By the end of the programme he demonstrated ability to initiate and respond to eye contact from others.
- The quality of John's social interaction with others changed. He was observed to anticipate and initiate as well as to respond. He developed the capacity to turn take and wait.
- John's communication became purposeful with choice making evident. There was evidence that John required significant lengths of time to enable him to process a request, plan a response and implement it.
- John demonstrated the ability to use shared (joint) attention, and was observed to indicate his needs by approaching staff and using gestural prompting to advocate his needs.
- John demonstrated the ability to generalise these skills.
- John became more adaptive to changes in his environment and to daily schedules during the programme.
- John's social environment expanded, with John choosing to sit in various rooms (living room and music room).
- John developed the ability to seek comfort from others when upset.
- John showed decreased incidences of specific target behaviours with an overall improvement in his level of communication obvious to all.

Throughout the sequence of video clips obtained, there was a sense of progression and skill development in John and in those supporting him. John's family reported positive changes in John, observing him to be responsive and interacting more with the world around him. They also reported that John would have been similar to this a number of years ago but seemed to have lost it somewhere along the line. This pilot study identifies the substantial influence John's social environment and opportunities for interaction have on his ability to develop his communication skills as well as his desire to communicate. John appeared to benefit from participation in the programme and it has significantly enhanced his quality of life. The implementation of Intensive Interaction has given John a framework of support to enable him to develop and communicate competencies and skills.

I feel through this case study, John has highlighted the importance of dropping our own objectives and adapting a more holistic approach to supporting communication to include facilitating social interaction and human connection with people with severe/profound intellectual disabilities. He has emphasised the impact Intensive Interaction can have on a person's overall communication development as well as their social and emotional wellbeing. Emotional wellbeing is closely associated with quality of life (Moss et al., 2000). I feel John identifies a need to re-evaluate our focus on prioritising task orientated, SMART objectives to the detriment of supporting social interaction and fostering relationships in residential settings. Addressing staff education and awareness on how to work together with the people we support, in finding ways to communicate and socially connect, that can enhance a sense of well being, promote self-advocacy and enhance relationships and emotions, needs to become a priority in policy making and practice.

References

Barber, M. (2012) Promoting Communication rather than Generating Data. In Hewett, D. (ed.). *Intensive Interaction. Theoretical Perspectives*. SAGE Publications: London, UK. pp. 88–103.

Bowlby, J., Fry, M. and Ainsworth, M.S.D. (1990) *Child Care and the Growth of Love*. 2nd edn. London, UK: Penguin Books.

Bowlby J. (1969) *Attachment. Attachment and Loss: Vol. 1*. New York, NY: Basic Books.

Bowlby, J. (1988) *A Secure Base: Clinical Implications of Attachment Theory*. London, UK: Routledge.

Firth, G., Berry, R. and Irvine, C. (2010) *Understanding Intensive Interaction Contexts and Concepts for Professionals and Families*. London, UK: Jessica Kingsley Publishers.

Goleman, D. (2004) *Emotional Intelligence & Working with Emotional Intelligence*. London, UK: Bloomsbury Publishing.

Health Information and Quality Authority (HIQA) (2013) National Standards for Residential Services for Children and Adults with Disabilities, Ireland.

Maslow, A.H. (1943) 'A Theory of Human Motivation.' *Psychological Review* 50(4), pp. 370–396.

Moss, S., Bouras, N. and Holt, G. (2000) 'Mental health services for people with intellectual disability: a conceptual framework.' *Journal of Intellectual Disability Research* 44(2), pp. 97–107.

Rogers, C.R. (1957) 'The necessary and sufficient conditions of therapeutic personality change.' *Journal of Consulting Psychology* 21(2), pp. 95–103.

Stern, D.N. (2000) *The Interpersonal World of the Infant. A View from Psychoanalysis and Developmental Psychology*. New York, NY: Basic Books.

Chapter 5

Less is more
Working with a person with PMLD

Amandine Mourière

This chapter focusses primarily on the importance of the essential Intensive Interaction technique of 'minimalism.' Amandine explains how Sarah helped her rethink her understanding of Intensive Interaction techniques. By doing less and less, not only did she see Sarah's communication develop greatly, but Amandine also became a better mentor for her colleagues. This chapter also offers rich detail on how to record progress, as well as reflective practice in action.

Background story: my experience of Intensive Interaction

I first encountered Intensive Interaction five years ago, whilst working as a teaching assistant in a special needs school. At the time, I was working in a class with children who all had a diagnosis of classic autism. The daily routine was highly structured, and the teaching style was directive throughout the whole day. As a consequence, the occurrences of challenging behaviours were way too frequent, and both staff and pupils suffered from it. I was not happy with the way things were and Intensive Interaction came like a revelation. Not only could I see benefits in the children's communication skills, but I also immediately felt at ease with the approach. The responsive nature of Intensive Interaction, its gentleness and respect for the other person's behaviours made me feel confident and reassured. Because the approach is person-centred, the free will and free expression of the other person are respected (Guthrie, 2009), and each and everyone's personality is celebrated and valued (Department of Health, 2009, p. 34). I quickly realised how Intensive Interaction could be implemented in everything we did at school, and used throughout the whole day. I felt that the approach was extremely respectful of the other person, as well as holistic; whilst Intensive Interaction aims at developing a person's communication skills, it often impacts on other areas of development as well.

I soon realised that support from my class teacher was essential. However, our views on the matter differed so much I ended up in a tricky position: on the one hand, I knew Intensive Interaction was the way forward, and that it could truly make a difference in connecting and bonding with these children ... but on the other hand I was unable to rationally explain why, to argue against other methods. My teacher's main argument was to mention her teaching degree in special needs, and therefore her better understanding of autism; she kept saying that I did not see the whole picture. Intensive Interaction can look so lovely and playful, that it may be seen as a light-hearted add-on to the day, a time-filler. What is more, the naturalistic nature of the approach – based on the infant-caregiver model (Schaffer, 1977) – tends to not give it full credit, as if it was too simple, too developmentally sensitive. In a nutshell, my lack of technical knowledge in explaining the rationale and the benefits of Intensive Interaction meant that I was not being taken seriously.

I am a true believer in following your instinct ... unfortunately it is sometimes not quite enough to convince other people.

Studying for a master's degree

Between my passion for autism, and my belief in Intensive Interaction, I decided to enrol for a master's degree in autism. I based all my assignments on people at early levels of development, and wrote my dissertation on the efficacy of Intensive Interaction on a child with a diagnosis of classic autism. I did not realise what I was letting myself into when I signed up for the course. The course was a challenge, in a number of different ways. The one challenge worth mentioning here, is that the more I was reading about autism and early levels of development, the less I felt I knew. And perhaps my biggest learning was that at the end of the day, academic knowledge needs to go hand in hand with practical work. Whilst I have broadened my knowledge and understanding of autism, each person is unique, and therefore the way we support them needs to reflect this reality; it is crucial to always keep a fresh eye, and never assume we understand it all. I would soon be confronted by this reality.

After I completed my master's, I finally felt I had the vocabulary and the arguments to defend the benefits, value, and crucial aspects of Intensive Interaction for people with autism.

I then enrolled on the Intensive Interaction Co-ordinator Course, which takes place over a period of 15 months. For the purpose of the course, each member is to select an individual they have regular access to, in order to record and assess the individual's progress as well as providing opportunities to reflect on their own practice and develop accordingly. However, just as I was to start my Co-ordinator Course, an unforeseen event was to challenge my newly acquired knowledge. I was assigned to a class with children with profound and multiple learning disabilities (PMLD).

Whilst very pleased to be working with this group of children and the lovely class team, I did wonder how I was supposed to do Intensive Interaction with someone with PMLD … how similar or different would it be to do Intensive Interaction? How much would I need to adapt? Would I need to do more in order to get a response? So many questions, which I was about to answer … with the help of Sarah.

Sarah: profile and description

This is how I met Sarah. She was one of the seven students in Dolphin Class. All the children in the class had profound and multiple learning difficulties, aged between 6 and 10 years old. When I started this project, Sarah was 9 years old. She has profound and multiple learning difficulties, she takes nil by mouth, and has cortical visual impairment (CVI), meaning that her brain does not process nor make sense of the information that her eyes capture.

After about a week in the class, she raised my interest and curiosity over the other pupils. Whilst far from being the most complex child in the class, Sarah certainly was the quietest, most isolated of all. She stood out almost immediately as the perfect candidate for this project. The other pupils would cry, vocalise, or use their body to communicate or reach out, Sarah did not seem to attempt any of this. She appeared to be 'switched off' much of the time. Consequently, Sarah seemed to have very little awareness and understanding of her peers and of her environment. As Melanie Nind puts it:

> 'to be effective communicators we have to want to communicate, to have a concept of what communication is all about, and to simultaneously apply many complex and inter-related skills.' (Nind, 1998, p. 98)

Did Sarah have a concept of communication? From my initial observation, she spent a lot of time on her own. Was it Sarah's choice, her inability to reach out, or staff not knowing how to connect with her? If Sarah knew how to reach out, and connect with her peers, would she still choose to spend so much time by herself? Was there anything we could do to teach her these skills? I wanted to enable Sarah to make that choice, and not remain in this kind of default position.

Initial observation, prior to starting Intensive Interaction

Observation is a major aspect of doing Intensive Interaction; it allows the practitioner 'to learn their person.' Even though you may have known an individual for a while, you will probably see them in a slightly different light with the Intensive Interaction technique and principles in mind. By sitting with your person and not doing very much, you can simply enjoy their company, and learn their behaviours and potential meanings (Hewett, 2012). This observational period allows you to tune-in better with your person; it helps discriminate between behaviours that may be conducive to having an interaction and those which may not be. It helps to think about how to best join in with them, and of when and how to respond to them.

When sitting in her chair, Sarah was restless and clearly looked unhappy. She was fidgety, grabbing anything at reach: her sling, cardigan, somebody else's hair, clothes ... the message was pretty clear 'Get me out of this chair!'

Sarah loves spending time on the floor; this is where she is at her happiest. Freedom of movement is crucial to her. When on the floor, she would sometimes have a smile on her face; she appeared to be content. Often her eyes would be fixated on the ceiling: with the class teacher – Julie, we speculated that Sarah was looking at the neon lights. She seemed completely absorbed by their brightness and seemed even less reachable then.

Sarah did not use any vocalisations, almost it seemed, as if unaware of her vocal chords. She smiled to express happiness and contentment, which would usually occur whilst on the mat, listening to music. When she had enough of being in her standing frame, or sitting in her chair, her face would deform and grimace.

Two of Sarah's behaviours appeared to have communicative functions, but I question how intentional and aware Sarah really was when producing these behaviours. I could only speculate on their significance, as any responses from an adult rarely seemed to soothe her or reach her. Putting her hand in her mouth seemed to signify that she was bored. Trying to grab anything at reach could mean that she needed to be active or to interact with someone.

- enjoying being with another person
- developing the ability to attend to that person
- concentration and attention span
- learning to do sequences of activity with another person
- taking turns in exchanges of behaviour
- sharing personal space
- using and understanding eye contact
- using and understanding facial expressions
- using and understanding physical contacts
- using and understanding non-verbal communication
- using vocalisations with meaning
- learning to regulate and control arousal level

Figure 5.1 The fundamentals of communication.

From these initial observations, it became clear that Sarah was still at a very early level of development. Looking at the Fundamentals of Communication list (FOCs, Nind & Hewett, 2001) only reinforced my initial observations: Sarah had very little knowledge and performance in being a communicator.

Starting up

At the beginning, I had to think of the best environment and time to do Intensive Interaction with Sarah. As often stressed on training, it can be necessary to timetable sessions when first starting Intensive Interaction with an individual. There are three reasons for this: first, to make sure time is protected during the day, secondly for the person to learn this new way of being and interacting, and finally to give the practitioner time to build confidence. Ultimately, Intensive Interaction becomes the normal, natural way to communicate and interact, and will naturally spill over into all areas and throughout the whole day.

For someone like Sarah, at such an early level of development, getting to that place is going to take time. It was very clear from the start that she would need consistent daily sessions with one main interactive partner at first, in order to develop some awareness and understanding of the whole process.

It was agreed with the class teacher Julie, that I would do Intensive Interaction with Sarah first thing in the morning. Thus, a new routine was introduced: as soon as Sarah came in in the morning, I used to hoist her onto the mat, let her stretch for 5–10 minutes, and I would then join her, and spend between 20 to 30 minutes with her.

Minimalism

I was extremely fortunate to be working with a supportive class team. Everything seemed to be in my favour. Above all, the class teacher played an important role in this. Julie was very supportive of the approach as well as of my course; she facilitated my project as best as possible; everything fell into place very smoothly and easily.

And yet … the biggest challenge I was to face did not come from external forces, but from within. Doing Intensive Interaction with a person with PMLD was new to me. Even though I felt I was very much tuned-in with Sarah, I was joining-in with her behaviours, and responding to them, it did not seem to be very conducive at first. I felt I was not getting through to her. What is more, I could not tell whether she was aware of my presence or not.

I came to the conclusion that even though I was applying the techniques, my style needed some adjustments. By reviewing the videos, I soon realised that I was trying too hard; I was joining-in with too many of Sarah's behaviours, and therefore was probably further confusing her rather than helping her develop awareness of my presence. Moreover, some of my responses were too complex at times, and would just add to the confusion. In one instance, a nursery rhyme CD was playing in the background; I was so desperate to get Sarah's attention that I started whistling over the song playing – 'The Wheels on the Bus'. Try to picture this scenario for a minute: Sarah is on the mat, moving her arms and legs, smiling at the music, whilst I am lying next to her joining-in with her movements and whistling over the music. It is pretty clear that I was doing too much, way too much. My style seriously needed to be stripped down and re-focused in these ways:

– **Tuning-in:** I needed to take my time more, observe the behaviours which were worth joining-in with. Observing Sarah more, being with her rather than doing with her.

- **Joining-in:** identifying the behaviours that would be conducive to interacting with Sarah, to get a sense of togetherness.
- **Responding:** can prove to be a tricky aspect of technique in Intensive Interaction. How to respond, when to respond…this aspect would very much depend on how tuned-in I was with Sarah, and what behaviours I chose to join-in with.

In a nutshell, I was learning a crucial technique of Intensive Interaction:

- **MINIMALISM** – Don't do too much.
- Be responsive rather than directive.
- Build the content and the flow of the activity by responding to, and building on the behaviours of the learner.

There is another crucial consideration I needed to integrate into my practice. Are there any differences doing Intensive Interaction with someone with PMLD? There is one major difference – the brain. Someone with PMLD usually has extensive damage to their brain, and therefore will often present with neurological processing delays as well as significant physical and sensory impairments. However, whilst the effect of brain damage restricts the number of neurons as well as the numbers of synapses that can develop, synapses are formed throughout our lives due to brain plasticity. Thus, *'there are always possibilities that people with PMLD can make new connections and learn new things just like typically developing people'* (Lacey, 2009, p. 16). When it comes to doing Intensive Interaction, the techniques remain the same, as Intensive Interaction adapts, practitioners **adapt by tuning-in.** However, to be successful, the practitioner needs to be extremely **SLOW,** and adapt to the tempo of the learner.

As soon as I really, properly adjusted my tempo to Sarah's much, much slower one, she was switched on, and could eventually take part in the interaction.

Recording

In accordance with the course requirements, I used record sheets, video-recordings, and progress-tracks to record Sarah's progress.

The **record sheets** were used to describe sessions. Noting any significant occurrences allowed me to self-evaluate and therefore adjust my practice accordingly for future sessions. Any comments or thoughts for future sessions were also jotted down.

The first record sheet below (Figure 5.2) on the left refers to the very first Intensive Interaction session I had with Sarah. What strikes me is that I was already aware that I was doing too much by being directive at times. However, it took me a few weeks to figure out how I needed to change and adapt for the interaction to be successful. The second record sheet (Figure 5.3) says it all. I'll list the changes that occurred in a six weeks' time span:

- **Sarah's positioning**: she was often unhappy in her chair, restless and fidgety. I therefore prioritised time when Sarah was on the floor.
- **Background noise**: whenever music was on, I could not tell whether Sarah was connecting and responding to me, or to the music. After discussing this issue with the class team, we decided to make sure there was no music when I was carrying out Intensive Interaction with Sarah.

Interaction Session Sheet

Student: Sarah   Date: 14/01/14   Staff: Amandine

Description of Session:

Sarah was in her chair & I was sitting on her left hand-side. Lots of head movements as well as arms? Ended the interaction by falling asleep.

Significant Occurrences: particularly anything new that happened

Sarah grabbed my hand a couple of times & moved it. She also gave me a few sustainable eye-contacts. Responded to blowing on her hand.

Try to evaluate your performance. What did you do that that successful and/or unsuccessful? How did you feel and why?

Found it difficult to find something that would interest/motivate her. I perhaps tried to hard to find something & did not give her enough time to process.

Other comments or observations, thoughts for the future

Still getting to know her. Take my time... let her teach me little by little. Perhaps not in her chair... on the mat?

Figure 5.2 Intensive Interaction Record Sheet 1.

Interaction Session Sheet

Student: Sarah   **Date:** 26/02/14   **Staff:** Amandine

Description of Session:

On the mats. No music, only 2 other children being fed so very quiet.
1st session after half-term.
→ kicking game
→ moving arms together
→ blowing when face or hands near my face

Significant Occurrences: particularly anything new that happened

So tuned-in, even after being off for a week. New game : kicking game. Not new but Sarah has become more involved in it, more aware. So much fun!

Try to evaluate your performance. What did you do that that successful and/or unsuccessful? How did you feel and why?

No music in the background was good; I knew she was responding to our interaction & not something else. It helps both of us to tune-in with each other better.

Other comments or observations, thoughts for the future

Quiet background more conducive!

Figure 5.3 Intensive Interaction Record Sheet 2.

- **Lighting**: when lying on the mat, Sarah would stare at the neon lights the entire time, completely absorbed by their brightness. By turning the lights off whenever possible, Sarah was less distracted and had greater opportunities to have face to face interactions.
- **Being responsive rather than directive**: I dropped the damaging idea that someone with PMLD needs prompting most of the time. By carefully responding to some of Sarah's behaviours, we were able to build a repertoire of activities, which gradually developed.

By adapting the environment around Sarah and making it right for her, she was almost instantly able to connect.

As well as recording sessions on paper, I also shot regular **videos:**

- solo videos every other month
- regular videos of the sessions

This way of recording is by far the most powerful. Julie and I used to sit in the staffroom first thing in the morning and watch back the numerous videos of Sarah I had shot. Together we analysed my style, discussed what was working best, what needed to be adapted ... I am absolutely convinced that we would not have made the changes I listed above as quickly as we did without the videos.

What is more, the use of videos allowed us to record the tiniest little changes occurring in Sarah's behaviours. It helped us read Sarah better, and not miss out crucial details in the subtle changes that were taking place in her.

Progress Tracks are another useful way to record somebody's changes and progress over time. At first, there would be a couple of things written down for the whole month (see figure 5.4 and 5.5). After a few months, we needed an extra sheet to write down the rapid changes in Sarah's behaviour and communicative abilities (see figures 5.6 and 5.7).

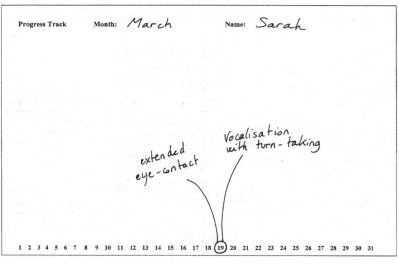

Figure 5.4 Intensive Interaction Progress Track 1.

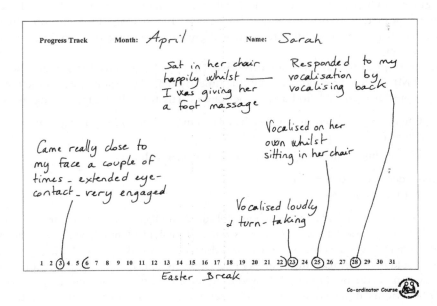

Figure 5.5 Intensive Interaction Progress Track 2.

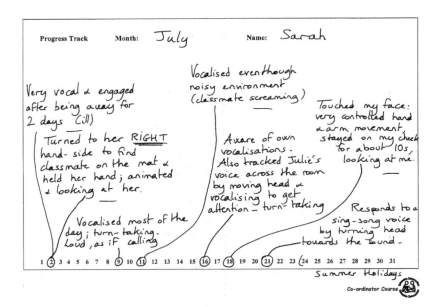

Figure 5.6 Intensive Interaction Progress Track 3.

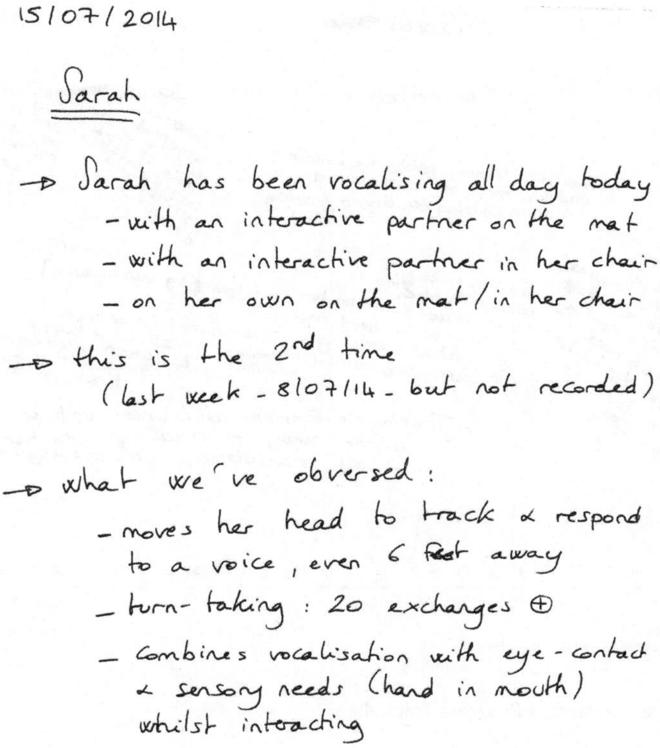

15 / 07 / 2014

<u>Sarah</u>

→ Sarah has been vocalising all day today
— with an interactive partner on the mat
— with an interactive partner in her chair
— on her own on the mat / in her chair

→ this is the 2nd time
(last week - 8/07/14 - but not recorded)

→ what we've observed :
— moves her head to track & respond
to a voice, even 6 feet away
— turn-taking : 20 exchanges ⊕
— combines vocalisation with eye-contact
& sensory needs (hand in mouth)
whilst interacting

Figure 5.7 Intensive Interaction: further notes to Progress Track 3.

A number of factors explain the increased use of the Progress Tracks:

- Daily Intensive Interaction input with one key person provided Sarah with security, safety and familiarity. Therefore, as she developed awareness, trust, and self-confidence, she was able to learn more use of the fundamentals of communication, which enabled her to reach out and communicate.
- Over time, Sarah increasingly understood she was in charge of the interaction, and increasingly initiated. Our repertoire of activities expanded, and through the repetition of the activities, Sarah became more aware, more confident, and ultimately displayed subtle changes as well as very obvious ones.
- Finally, the whole class team was involved, and together we learnt to observe Sarah, to question, share, discuss … and we soon agreed that anyone in the class would record Sarah's progress using the Progress Track. I felt it was a good way to keep everyone involved and learn to observe small but significant progress. Three of us were mainly involved in the recording process: the class teacher Julie, Hanan and I (both teaching assistants). The two other members of staff would feedback to us though, and that helped us keep the momentum going (see Figure 5.8).

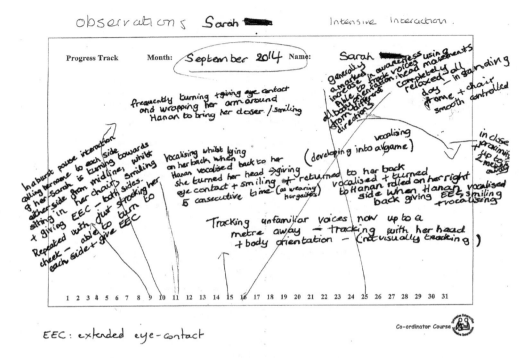

Figure 5.8 Intensive Interaction Progress Track 4.

Spill over and Sarah's progress

Observing someone sounds like an easy thing to do… believe me, it is not! What are you actually looking for? I believe that one needs to carefully consider what is to be observed, and develop the art of seeing. For someone at such an early level of development, changes in their abilities to communicate and relate may be minute. Learning to see and be rewarded by tiny things is absolutely crucial. If the practitioner fails to recognise and respond to new communication attainments, the learner is likely to lose them straight away. *'By sensitive watching and waiting, synchronized interaction sequences can be achieved, leading to joint attention and sometimes to turn-taking routines'* (Kellett, 2004, p. 178). Here, through attributing intentionality to Sarah's actions, I was supporting the transition to intentional communication (Harding, 1983). Therefore, Intensive Interaction could be described as a free-play approach in which the practitioners join-in the play *'so that they can enhance the play and thus the learning'* (Lacey cited in Hewett, 2012, p. 47).

In the present scenario, I wanted to observe Sarah's communicative abilities, and changes overtime. It can prove to be a tricky task when you are dealing with someone who is non-verbal, and does not reach out very much.

In order to help me in this process, I based my observations on the three main senses a person at early levels of development is likely to use in order to communicate (based on the FOCAL wheels, Mourière, 2017).

My initial observations of Sarah were:

Visual/gestural:
> Very little awareness
> Visually impaired therefore not sure what she sees, and when
> Looks at the lights when on the mat, mesmerised

Vocal/auditory:
> No vocalisation noticed
> Often smiles when the music is on

Tactile:
> Grimaces when has enough of standing
> Needs freedom of movement
> When on the floor, moves about a lot, and sometimes she shows awareness of another
> person at reach

After 6 weeks:

Visual/gestural:
> Seems to be more aware of her interactive partner
> Seeks to look at her interactive partner by rolling to side when on the mat
> More aware of her gestures (kicking, grabbing), and of sharing activities involving
> movement

Vocal/auditory:
> The odd vocalisation at times, but does not seem to be intentional, or to be aware it
> comes from her
> Recognizes familiar voices and responds to them by moving towards the person,
> smiling

Tactile:
> Shows increasing awareness of her interactive partner's presence. Sarah has
> become more confident and has started to explore the person next to her through
> touch
> Grabs hands, or arms
> Kicks her legs about, and clearly enjoys the 'kicking game'

After 12 weeks:

Visual/gestural:
> Lots of extended eye-contact, especially when she is on the mat
> Definitely sees at times!
> Tends to bring her face very close to mine, as if to 'scrutinise me'
> Often puts a hand on me when I am lying next to her
> Often holds my hand

Vocal/auditory:

> More vocal than ever before, and louder
> Vocalizes and turn-takes sometimes
> Recognizes my voice and tunes-in

Tactile:

> Often seeks my presence when on the mat, and puts a hand on my face or holds my hand
> Not as fidgety as before, seems to be more in control of her movements

After 18 weeks:

Visual/gestural:

> Extended eye-contact, not only on the floor but also in her chair or standing-frame
> Scrutinises my face when in very close proximity with hers
> On the mat, Sarah reaches out to grab my hands, pulls herself onto her side, and looks at me smiling
> Attempts to feel my face, and does so with some help

Vocal/auditory:

> Extremely vocal at times, but not consistent
> Turn-taking and growing awareness

Tactile:

> More settled, in control of her limbs
> Holds hands when on the mat, attempts to feel my face, my arms
> Likes to kick her feet and turn-takes

Summary of Sarah's progress

Visual/gestural modality

Sarah had very little awareness when we first started Intensive Interaction. Because of the way she presented, the team believed that Sarah was unable to see. Even when she seemed to look at somebody's eyes, it felt as if she was seeing 'through' the person.

After 12 weeks, Sarah started to show emerging awareness of eye contact. The team working with her reached an agreed judgement that she was now aware of my presence and could see me at times. She also started to use simple gestures by putting a hand on me when I was lying next to her, and by holding my hand sometimes.

At 18 weeks, Sarah's use of eye contact and simple gestures clearly became increasingly intentional through the quality of the interactions. She would attempt to feel my face, or reach out to grab my hand. The quality of her eye contacts dramatically changed too. I can only speculate that her eyes started to process what they were seeing, as Sarah started to make sense of the world. Ospina (2009) observes that by *'reducing the amount of visual stimulation by presenting simple rather than crowded visual environments is believed to enhance vision in children who have CVI. Cueing by language, touch [...] are among the many useful strategies for optimizing residual vision'* (p. 87).

At 10 months, Sarah would frequently turn onto her side and give prolonged eye-contact for up to 20 seconds at a time, looking away and looking back. The team also noticed how her movements became more controlled and she would gently touch her interactive partner's face and search to hold a hand.

At 12 months, Sarah recognised the use of eye-contact as a way to communicate and relate. The staff also observed that Sarah started to transfer and generalise these skills to environments other than the floor.

Tactile

Sarah made the most progress in the tactile/haptic modality, starting from very little awareness at baseline, to being able to recognise, respond, and engage in communicating through the use of touch.

Between the baseline assessment and 12 weeks into taking part in Intensive Interaction activities, Sarah went from 'moves her arms a lot and explores things at reach' to 'seems to be seeking my presence when I am close to her' and 'not as fidgety, more in control of her movements.'

At 18 weeks, there is a noticeable leap in Sarah's understanding and use of touch in order to communicate and relate; 'more settled, in control of her limbs,' 'hold hands when on the mat, attempts to feel my face,' 'likes to kick her feet and started to turn-take.'

At 10 months, Sarah made further progress 'gently touching Hanan's face,' 'very still and calm,' 'turned to Hanan, rolled on her right side' (when she would only ever turn onto her left).

The 12 months' assessment does not show further progress on the FOCAL wheels, but Sarah still continued making progress, further developing and polishing the skills she had been learning for the past year; 'finding and holding Hanan's hand', 'gently touching Hanan's face', 'putting both arms around Hanan's neck and pulling Hanan towards her.'

Vocal/auditory

At baseline, Sarah had very little awareness of her voice and did not seem to pay attention to people's voices. However, I noted that she 'responds to music by smiling and moving about.'

Twelve weeks later, Sarah's awareness of her own voice as well as of her interactive partner started to develop. She then started to vocalise, which would hardly ever happen prior to starting Intensive Interaction, and 'recognise my voice and tune-in with me.'

At 18 weeks, the FOCAL wheels show very little progress, but I noted that 'Sarah is extremely vocal at times', 'not consistent', and 'turn-taking and growing awareness.'

Ten months in, Sarah's vocal communication became increasingly intentional as well as her awareness and ability to attend to someone else's voice; 'vocalised and turned to Hanan, rolled back and forth from back to side, and acknowledged Hanan vocalising back to her by smiling and vocalising again.'

At 12 months, whilst the FOCAL wheels do not show any difference, the Progress Tracks describe how Sarah carried on making progress and consolidated the skills recently acquired; 'vocalised throughout the whole day, and developed into a turn-taking conversation whilst sat in her chair,' 'responding to my voice by vocalising, looking, smiling and turning towards'.

Pupil name, year group, date of admission, gender, date	*Use first name only or Pupil SK*	
Date of placement on SEN record and current SEN status		FSM Y/N

Pen Portrait including area(s) of need (COP) *circle and prioritise area of need/s*

    CLN   BESD   CIN   SPN

SK has PMLD and complex medical needs. SK communicates using fleeting eye contact, smiling and she will cry if uncomfortable or in pain. Sk follows a daily positional and mobility programme to ensure her well being and enable access to the curriculum. Sk will play independently by tapping and swiping toys. Sk is learning to anticipate repetitively presented stimuli. Sarah presents as passive and having a limited awareness of herself in relation to significant others. It was observed that she would benefit from using intensive interaction as the main approach to developing her early communication skills.

Attendance data: Good attendance
Current
Previous

PROVISION OVER TIME / ARRANGEMENTS OVER TIME

Intervention

Over a six month period daily at least one to one intensive interaction to develop Sarah's early communication skills.
These were initially with one member of the team who is an intensive interaction practitioner.
Training was given by myself and Amandine on how to observe and record progress and create a responsive environment.
A baseline assessment using video evidence and detailed observational notes was taken in February 2014. Weekly detailed observational notes were taken using weekly video evidence to track and record progress. As Sarah's communication skills developed al members of the team engaged with her regularly using the same approach.

How the skills of staff have been developed to address needs	The class team were trained on how to effectively interact with S to promote her communication skills. This was done by modelling the approach and mentoring individuals. The approach was also used as the main approach to effectively develop the communication skills of other pupils in the class group. The class team quickly became confident at using this approach naturally throughout the school day to enhance the learning environment and communication skills of Sarah and other pupils in the class.

IMPACT										**QUANTITATIVE OUTCOMES FOR PUPIL**								
YEAR										July 2012			July 2013			Oct 2014		
Attainment P levels	sp	lis	cit	sp.	lis	cit	sp	lis	cit	sp	lis	cit	sp	lis	cit	sp	lis	cit
	PIi	PIi	PIi	PIi	PIi	PIi	PIii	PIii	PIii	PIii	PIii	PIii	PIii	PIii	PIii	P2i	P2i	P2i

<u>Progress Summary</u>   sp and lis – speaking and listening
                     cit - citizenship
      A recent assessment, October 2014, has shown SK to have progressed from PIii to P2i in Communication.
      This was using the recently redrafted Communication Profound Curriculum assessment tool.
      A detailed case study file tracks SK's progress over time. In the citizenship aspect of the PSHCE curriculum SK has Progressed from PIii to P2i as assessed in October 2014

Figure 5.9 Case study of a pupil with special education needs (SEN).

IMPACT	QUALITATIVE OUTCOMES FOR PUPIL

Independence/ confidence / attitude to learning

- SK will maintain an interaction for up to twenty minutes with all the adults in class
- During these interaction she will give prolonged eye contact up to 15 seconds, use a wide range of facial expressions and iniate and interaction by turning towards an adult and reaching out to gently touch them.
- SK will now have a turn taking conversation with an adult using her own sounds for up to five turns each.
- SK is much more aware of her learning environment. For example she is responding to familiar voices spontaneously by smiling, turning towards and sometimes vocalising.
- As soon as you speak to SK she will respond by turning towards you, smiling and giving sustained eye contract.
- SK will now vocalise in different contexts and situation.

Social skills / relationships–peers and adults

- SK enjoys interacting with all the adults in class
- SK is much calmer and more fluid and controlled in her gross motor movements
- SK now initiates and maintains a social and communicative interactions familiar adult
- SK is more aware and alert of her learning environment

Other

Parents have observed Sarah is more communicative alert and interactive. This was recorded at SK's annual review

Impact on wider school practice and provision All staff feel that this approach has enhanced SK's communication skills and emotional well being

Figure 5.10 Case study with a pupil with SEN verso.

Mentoring

Halfway through the Co-ordinator Course, each member chooses a colleague to mentor. Between block 4 and block 7, not only our practices are being shared and evaluated with the rest of the group, but also our abilities to mentor somebody else and support them in developing their practice.

I chose to mentor my class teacher Julie, for a number of reasons. First, working alongside each other was extremely convenient. Secondly, Julie was already a great believer in Intensive Interaction, and understood the principles and the rationale of the approach. Lastly, we both wanted to concentrate on one particular pupil in the class, but had difficulties in knowing how to proceed, therefore bouncing ideas off each other's experiences was the best way to move forward and actually learn together.

The mentee is asked to follow a similar journey to their mentor. After selecting a person, regular videos are shot and written notes completed. It is crucial for the mentor to have regular contact with their mentees, and evaluate videos of each other's practices

My mentoring experience with Julie was split between two pupils: Sarah and Manpreet. The main reason for this was that I pretty much knew what I was doing with Sarah at that point, and therefore I could mentor Julie to the best of my abilities. In Manpreet's case, we were both very much at the same starting point, not quite knowing where to start.

Manpreet's profile

Manpreet was six years old at the time. She has a diagnosis of profound and multiple learning disabilities, she is deaf and visually impaired. She has very limited movements and can only move her head and fingers slightly. Manpreet has great difficulties breathing and needs suction on a daily basis: she has a one to one medical carer at all times. Manpreet's health deteriorated a couple of months prior to starting the mentoring project, and she then needed a constant supply of oxygen. Due to Manpreet's high physical needs, we did not know how to access her and the class team felt that she probably was the most isolated child in the school.

Starting Intensive Interaction with Manpreet

Whilst both Julie and I knew that Intensive Interaction was the way forward to accessing Manpreet, we were not quite sure how to proceed at first. We spent a considerable amount of time discussing the 'how' to do Intensive Interaction with Manpreet. It soon became clear that there was only one channel we could use to access her: touch, the 'mother of all senses' (Montagu, 1971). If Manpreet cannot hear, see, or vocalise, we had to reach her through the tactile modality. However, even though it felt right to go down this path, I was also very conscious of the need to back up my feelings with some actual research to support what seemed to be a rather unusual way to work with a pupil. Also, I was hoping that this project with Manpreet could help write up guidelines and support a curriculum through touch for other pupils as complex as her. I started looking for research on touch, and Dave Hewett directed me to a number of books and articles that would help me. I started to frenetically read everything I could find on the subject, and would then share it with the class team. Quickly, the whole team was on board and we used every single opportunity to discuss the importance of using touch with Manpreet, and how we would then proceed.

A session with Manpreet

We had to carefully plan sessions with Manpreet. Due to her physical needs, Manpreet would spend most of the day on the achiever (learning station which very much resembles a bed). She could spend some time on the floor, but needed a member of staff with her at all times, which needed careful planning due to the other children's needs. We all agreed that at first, I would model Intensive Interaction with Manpreet. I wrote a detailed programme on what a session should look like for Manpreet. Both Julie and I felt that it was crucial we wrote everything down, for two main reasons: for consistency so Manpreet would feel safe and secure, and develop an awareness and understanding of the situation, and because I was to work in a different class a month later so staff could carry on similarly with her.

A session would therefore look like this:

- Hoisting Manpreet onto the floor, on the mats
- Laying behind her to feel her whole body
- Having a mirror in front of Manpreet's face to monitor any facial expressions, or movements
- Joining-in with Manpreet's breathing by breathing back against her cheek, with one hand on her chest or on her own hand

Mentoring Julie with Manpreet

Every step of the way was discussed with Julie. I only had one month working alongside her before the end of the school year, and I already knew we would not be working together the next year. However, after explaining the circumstances to the head teacher, it was agreed that I would swap with a member of staff from Julie's class one morning a week to keep mentoring her. Spending time in the class proved to be quite difficult: either Manpreet was not in or there was a staff issue that prevented me from swapping with a member of staff. Julie and I still managed to spend time discussing Manpreet and reviewed videos together during our breaks.

Mentoring someone as experienced and knowledgeable as Julie was not always an easy task. I was extremely fortunate that Julie has no problem reflecting on herself and would always be open to discussion. She never took anything personally, and we learnt a lot together. With retrospect, I feel that we were both each other's mentees, as we learnt together and grew together through the use and implementation of Intensive Interaction in Dolphin class.

Mentoring Hanan: my biggest learning curve

I shall end this chapter with a small paragraph about Hanan, as her journey through Intensive Interaction was my greatest lesson of all.

Hanan and I both started to work in Julie's class around the same time, shortly after I was to start my Co-ordinator Course, and my daily routine with Sarah had started. Hanan would sometimes ask me what I was doing with Sarah: 'are you working on her eyesight?' she would ask, or 'you should do some tracking lights with her, she can do it you know?!' I had great difficulties explaining to Hanan what I was doing with Sarah, but as a Co-ordinator-to-be I felt I had a responsibility in trying at the least.

I struggled at first, as part of me just wanted to be in my bubble. However, I did my best to always answer her questions, without any judgements, and would share with her Sarah's progress and explain why, always emphasising to her the technicalities of Intensive Interaction rather than on my own practice. By doing so, Hanan's confidence started to grow and soon enough she was giving it a go herself.

Hanan was doing it almost secretively, and I did not make a fuss about this at first: she was starting to change her practice, from years of directiveness to this very gentle and responsive approach. Not doing too much was hard for Hanan, but I could see her actively and consciously trying to apply the newly discovered concept of such minimalism. I started to feel quite excited about it though, and one day I shot a video of her having a chat with Sarah. I did not tell her at first. When she became aware I was filming her, she felt rather self-conscious but her smile was enough to encourage me to carry on. At the end of that day, I played the video on the computer and highlighted all the good techniques Hanan was using with Sarah, and their potential benefits on Sarah's development and well-being. Hanan was starting to grasp it, and from then on, there was no stopping her. She would ask me questions which sometimes proved to be challenging, she would ask me what to read … she became so enthused she wanted to tell everyone about it! After I left Dolphin class, Hanan made sure all the children in the class were getting their amount of chit-chat on a daily basis. She also made it her mission to work closely with Manpreet, and would model for other staff whilst bringing to their attention the importance of doing Intensive Interaction.

Hanan's journey is lovely and inspiring … but above all her journey ought to be seen as a lesson for all of us practitioners. I have met other 'Hanans' in my career, but she is the first one I did not dismiss right there on the spot. Through the Co-ordinator Course, I have learnt to be confident about my practice, rather than stay in my corner and do my thing. Hanan was curious and wanted to understand, even though she was being challenged by this new way of being with the children. Instead of feeling threatened, I welcomed her comments, questions, and doubts without judgment. If we want our colleagues to experience the wonders and benefits of Intensive Interaction for themselves, we need to apply the very same principles of Intensive Interaction: tuning-in with them, and joining them where they are at.

Thank you Hanan.

References

Department of Health (2009) *Valuing People Now: A New Three-year Strategy for People with Learning Disabilities*, HMSO, London.

Guthrie, N. (2009) 'Intensive interaction co-ordinator course'. *The Intensive Interaction Newsletter* 29, p. 2.

Harding, C. (1983) Setting the stage for language acquisition: Communication development in the first year. In: Golinkoff, R. (ed.). *The Transition from Pre-linguistic to Linguistic Communication*. New Jersey, NJ: Lawrence Erlbaum Associates. pp. 93–113.

Hewett, D. (2012) Preparing for Intensive Interaction. In Hewett, Firth, G., Barber, D., Harrison, T. (ed.). *The Intensive Interaction Handbook*. London, UK: SAGE Publications. pp. 29–44.

Kellett, M. (2004) 'Intensive interaction in the inclusive classroom: Using interactive pedagogy to connect with students who are hardest to reach.' *Westminster Studies in Education* 27(2). pp. 175–188.

Lacey, P. (2009) 'Developing the Thinking of Learners with PMLD. In Sharing Perspectives.' *PMLD Link,* 21(63). pp. 16–19.

Lacey, P. (2012) Interactive approaches to teaching and learning. In Hewett, D. (ed.). *Intensive Interaction Theoretical Perspectives*. London, UK: SAGE. pp. 39–54.

Montagu. A. (1971) *Touching: The human significance of the skin*. 2nd ed. New York, NY: Columbia University Press.

Mourière, A. (2017) 'Measuring the impact of intensive interaction on joint attention and intentional communication using the FOCAL wheels.' *Good Autism Practice* 18(1), pp. 34–45.

Nind, M. (1998) 'Intensive interaction and autism: A useful approach?' *British Journal of Special Education* 26(2), pp. 96–102.

Nind, M. and Hewett, D. (2001) *A Practical Guide to Intensive Interaction*. Kidderminster, UK: British Institute of Learning Disabilities.

Ospina, L.H. (2009) 'Cortical visual impairment', *Pediatrics in Review* 30(11), pp. 81–90.

Schaffer, R. (1977) *Mothering, the Developing Child*. London, UK: Harvard University Press.

Chapter 6

Building an emotional connection through Intensive Interaction

Lucy Hankin

In this chapter, Lucy explores the development of emotions. She relates how her practice developed hand in hand with Vincent's gradual abilities to connect with her and build psychological and emotional bridges. She talks with clarity about her journey to deepen her understanding of Intensive Interaction, and then to expand the knowledge and use of the approach within her school environment.

Developing an emotional connection with Vincent

Time for a different 'intervention'

Vincent was seven years old and had been at the school for around a year. He experienced a variety of interventions, including PECS (Picture Exchange Communication System), as well as the use of TEACCH (Treatment and Education of Autistic and Communication related Handicapped CHildren) to help structure his day. These interventions certainly helped Vincent learn to manage daily activities and to functionally communicate: he could complete tray tasks, sort shapes and colours correctly, even use a sentence strip to request motivating items ('I want trampoline'). However, something was still missing. There were still large periods of time where Vincent seemed difficult to reach and remained socially isolated.

It is acknowledged that the emotional well-being of people with autism is often neglected (Firth, Berry and Irvine, 2010). Sometimes this is a result of wrongful assumptions, for example, that there is an inherent inability for someone with autism to develop social and emotional engagement. Or, often, priority is placed on measurable outcomes to determine success at the expense of other essential learning: the most essential learning, of course, being the fundamentals of communication (Hewett, 2012b; see appendix 1). Therefore, it is important to challenge these assumptions: my journey with Vincent demonstrated the degree to which both social and emotional engagement is not only possible with a person with autism, but also integral to development and expression of self.

Developing my practice

Kellett, Nind and Mary (2003) discuss the importance of recognising practitioner progress in relation to pupil progress. During our Intensive Interaction journey, there were three key areas of my technique, which helped Vincent begin to engage socially, and eventually, emotionally: tuning-in, waiting/pausing, and responsiveness.

Getting to know Vincent: tuning-in takes time

I thought I knew Vincent fairly well, certainly in terms of likes (posting items, throwing balls, iPads, lining objects up, books), dislikes (moving away from preferred activities, getting messy, sand, changes to routine), and academic strengths and weaknesses. However, did this really mean that I knew Vincent? Put simply, no: these individual, superficial components could not simply be added together to get an idea of who Vincent is as a person.

Learning to tune-in to Vincent was something that developed over a fairly significant length of time: at the very least, several weeks of regular, often daily, observations and interactions. I had a very supportive teacher, who enabled these sessions to occur by not only releasing me for this purpose, but also ensuring they formed part of the class timetable.

Initially, I was very conscious of my attempts to tune-in but gradually, I became fluent in 'reading Vincent'. This process took time and lots of repetitions, particularly as the cues I was learning to read were extremely subtle, especially during initial interactions. I learnt to avoid the temptation to give up on sessions because nothing spectacular seemed to be happening. As I became able to tune-in subconsciously, I started to acknowledge the more subtle cues, for example, the fleeting glances that showed that Vincent was paying attention to me, but at that time, needed me to simply be there with him.

Learning to pause

As I became more proficient at tuning-in to Vincent, I gradually developed the ability to recognise pauses in the interaction, and to resist the urge to 'drive on', or do something to make 'something' happen.

Initially, this was hard! There were often sessions where for twenty or thirty minutes Vincent would lie down and look at his reflection in the mirror, tolerating my presence but only fleetingly acknowledging it with a glance. I'd love to say that I never gave in, but there were definitely occasions where I did too much and learnt the hard way: Vincent would move away, either physically, or emotionally, withdrawing into himself and the 'magic' of the session would be broken.

By having plenty of regular opportunities to interact, my practice developed as a result: I became less hurried, more relaxed and learnt to appreciate the pauses in our interactions as just that, pauses, rather than seeing them as gaps that needed filling. This meant that Vincent was able to use this time to process the interaction, and also it allowed him to take the lead.

Putting it into practice: the importance of pausing

Vincent comes to sit down by me, with his back to me, but sort of side on. We have a lovely sequence of turn-taking vocalisations, where I imitate but expand slightly on his sounds, using a conversational style. Each time I do this, Vincent giggles, smiling and giving me brief eye contact. After a couple of minutes, he makes a different sound, which I imitate: louder with a different tone; his facial expression changes to a 'quieter' one and he looks away but we remain in contact, forehead to forehead. There is a good twenty seconds here where 'nothing' seems to happen. During this time, I wait: still there, still available, but without driving on. Then, slowly, a smile creeps across his face and into his eyes and he opens his face up to me: I respond by opening my face too, smiling and opening my mouth and lifting my face in response to his. I am rewarded with a return to a sequence of turn-taking vocalisations, lit up by the most beautiful smile and laugh (reflection from a session sheet).

I cannot stress how important it was that I gave Vincent that pause: pausing is an important way of processing the quite complex activities in the interaction (Hewett, 2012b). By allowing Vincent this time, it meant he could process what had happened so far, but crucially allowed him to continue to take the lead, retaining the flow of the interaction.

When copying became responding

Initially, I focussed too much on copying as a technique: I didn't realise that this meant that although we had some lovely interactions, I was missing opportunities to develop our repertoire. Watching video footage of our sessions helped me to realise this, as well as watching other good Intensive Interaction practice. Of course, this realisation also came as I began to tune-in more naturally to Vincent.

I began to change the way in which I conceptualised what I was doing: I started to think in terms of responding rather than copying. I would ask myself 'how does Vincent need me to respond?' Tuning-in, particularly to the combination of facial expression, vocalisation, movement and touch helped to guide me and shape my response. This also meant that rather than limiting my technique to copying, I thought about a greater range of techniques that came under the umbrella of responsiveness: copying/imitation, joining-in, gentle dramatisation, use of commentary, even 'holding' my available face and waiting.

This allowed Vincent to lead the interactions more fully, taking an active role in the session as I let myself be guided by him. As a result, I began to see many of the fundamentals of communication beginning to develop.

Vincent: important breakthroughs

Vincent begins to use touch to create a connection

Vincent has always been relatively tactile in our sessions, but initially his use of touch could be quite rough, forceful – to either bring me closer to him or to push me away. After a few months, I noticed Vincent had begun to use touch in a subtler way, to express trust and create a connection. Through watching one of my videos, I noticed as Vincent was walking past he would gently touch his hand on my arm in an affectionate way: it was his way of keeping in contact with me as he moved around the room.

As this emotional connection continued to grow, the way that he used touch also developed a further fluency as Vincent developed it alongside other fundamentals of communication: understanding facial expressions and using eye contact. This contributed to the overall sense of emotional connection within the interactions. Vincent was using touch in a gentle way to express emotions and a sense of caring, not only to create a connection, but also to maintain and develop it.

Expanding and showing understanding of facial expressions

Not only did the range of Vincent's facial expressions expand over the course of our journey but also, the purposefulness of them changed. Vincent began to take more notice of both his own facial expressions and mine. Vincent began to pull faces in the mirror, paying close attention to his face. Then he would watch my face carefully as I imitated his expression, sometimes looking from the mirror to my face and then back again.

This demonstrated he was beginning to further identify with his own facial expressions and how they influence people around him.

As Vincent also explored his emotions through the sessions, his smiles and use of subtle facial language started working alongside more meaningful eye contact. I started to feel that his facial expressions were beginning to be used to convey developing emotions, particularly his identification of these emotions.

Vocalisations: learning to take turns

Vincent often used vocalisations to signal his enjoyment of a session, particularly once we had begun to establish a repertoire. I began to develop my technique of imitating so that I would make my responding vocalisation more conversational in style. This gradually led to the whole sequence of vocalisations becoming more conversational and Vincent began to show an awareness of this. I noticed that Vincent started to extend his vocalisation each time I imitated him, gradually getting higher and longer with each repetition, then lower at the end of the turn-taking sequence.

It was crucial that I was tuned-in to Vincent, as I knew then how to use imitation to enable turn-taking to take place, and develop his awareness. Had I not been tuned-in, my use of imitation would not have been conducive to establish this pattern of turn-taking. The reciprocal imitative game provided Vincent with information about how much I enjoyed his company and how similar we both were (Meltzoff, 1999), therefore establishing a sense of connection, complicity and understanding.

Initiating Intensive Interaction

One of the biggest breakthroughs was when Vincent began to initiate interactions in different circumstances. Our regular sessions were often in the same room, usually the Interactive room (with lights and bubble tubes) or the Sensory Integration room. This gave Vincent a solid, safe 'base' to build the interactions without a lot of the distractions from other areas of school. As Vincent's repertoire and our rapport increased within these interactions, he gradually began to initiate interactions in other parts of school and at other times of the day, even during our class residential.

During registration, I would sing our hello song to Vincent and shake hands. Gradually, Vincent began to reach out to me, put his arms around me, sit on my lap, vocalise, and smile; all the time giving beautifully intense eye contact.

Following this, Vincent began to use photos to request interactions: he would go to the timetable, find the photo of the Interactive room and bring it to me and go to the door.

Regulation of arousal levels

Vincent had always found it quite difficult to control his arousal levels, particularly in response to situations he didn't like, as well as when he was over-excited and unable to process these emotions. This often demonstrated itself in terms of sensory seeking behaviours, sometimes biting in frustration at a situation, or sometimes simply by seeking pressure by pressing his hand (or mine) to his chin and vocalising loudly.

To begin with, these behaviours still formed part of our sessions (with the exception of biting). Vincent would have periods of time where he would engage and interact with me, then seek sensory stimulation in some way, usually vocalising loudly, and turn away from me, with his hand pressed firmly to his chin. This usually seemed to happen when his arousal levels were increasing to the point where he became over-stimulated and this was his way of calming himself down.

Around three months from the start, I noted the first session where this didn't happen at all, and soon this disappeared from his repertoire.

There seemed to be two main reasons for this:

- Firstly, my technique had improved: I was able to tune-in and read the cues for when he was becoming over-aroused, and tailor my response accordingly. Rather than letting my vocalisations get higher with him, or using speech (I used to say 'gentle'), I began to use slight shifts of position or lowering the tone of my responding vocalisation as a response. This seemed to retain the flow of the interaction better.
- Secondly, Vincent had had many opportunities to practise regulating his levels by this point, as we had many repetitions of the interactions.

These two combined together meant that Vincent was beginning to regulate his arousal levels.

Emotional learning (Hewett, 2013)

In addition to the fundamentals of communication, it is generally acknowledged that emotional learning and a sense of connectedness also takes place as a result of Intensive Interaction (Firth et al., 2010).

Our Intensive Interaction journey built an emotional connection, which enabled Vincent to begin to develop skills identified as emotional learning. These are more difficult to identify as visible behaviours, as this complex learning often manifests in different and, often unexpected, ways for each individual.

The fundamentals of communication 2: emotional learning

- Knowing that others care, learning to care
- enjoying being with another person – connecting, bonding etc.
- Attachment, attunement
- Self-security, to feel safe, secure, calm
- Self-esteem, sense of self
- To identify own feelings & see same in others
- Gradually to understand feelings
- Trust stuff etc.
- Empathy, knowing/caring about how somebody else feels
- Right-hemisphere brain development (early emotional learning prepares areas of the brain for later, higher functions)

Figure 6.1 The fundamentals of communication 2

(based on various: Bowlby et al., 1953, Lamb et al, 2002, Schore, 2003)

Vincent runs across the room smiling and laughing, then sits with me, pulling himself onto my lap with my arms around him. He looks up at the ceiling, blinking and his eyes well up, he looks directly at himself in the mirror, then smiles, contentedly (reflection from a session sheet).

In comparison to a lot of our previous sessions, this session was a lot quieter, not as active, but in terms of emotional connection it was hugely significant. Vincent's emotional response to the interaction, followed by acknowledgment of this (seeing the emotion in himself in the mirror), was a visible example of the identification of his own feelings as well as recognition of sense of self. This, combined with many other moments through the session conveyed a sense of trust, calmness, even affection: a real sense of Vincent's enjoyment of social connection.

What did this mean for Vincent?

The development of both the fundamentals of communication and the corresponding emotional learning led to a greater expression of Vincent's sense of personhood. For Vincent, this meant he was not only beginning to enjoy social interactions, but he was also able to confidently and meaningfully communicate this enjoyment, initiating more and more interactions.

As he seemed more confident in his own identity, Vincent was able to build a relationship with not only myself, but with other members of staff and even pupils. Vincent became interested in interacting with familiar pupils; particularly those who tried to interact with him, whereas previously he had shown little interest, often moving away.

Intensive Interaction gave Vincent the opportunity to defy assumptions that suggest autism prevents a person from being social, or even enjoying social interactions. Vincent not only engaged in social interactions, but actively sought them out: a true example of what is possible when we focus on changing our practice, rather than changing the individual: Vincent wasn't so hard to reach after all.

Mentoring

As my journey with Vincent became established, I began another important journey: learning to mentor my colleagues. Although the journey of my colleagues was important, I learnt as much from this process as from working with Vincent. I realised that mentoring colleagues required many similar techniques to Intensive Interaction: pausing and allowing self-evaluation, tuning-in to their needs and fine-tuning my response in return.

I had two very enthusiastic and natural Intensive Interaction practitioners as mentees: Jacqui and Emily. We agreed to meet every couple of weeks to do some basic training, as they hadn't had any 'official' Intensive Interaction training.

Their Intensive Interaction projects would have two main aspects:

1   Observing and recording the progress of a young person
2   The development of their own technique as practitioners

Observing and recording the progress of the young person

Giving both mentees the responsibility of recording and observing progress with an individual, helped lead to a greater sense of motivation and engagement in the process. It was important, therefore, for me to ensure that my mentees had both the opportunity to interact regularly with the young person, as well as have access to session recording sheets. I also needed to ensure that the sessions could be filmed at regular intervals not only for the recognition of the learner's progress, but also for development of self-evaluation. I tried to make myself available to video their practice when possible, especially if I could see an interaction occurring naturally throughout the day.

Opportunities for interaction

Through discussions with the class teacher, we had some protected time for Intensive Interaction. Jacqui and Emily could therefore use this time to develop their practice, each with a specific pupil, although they worked with others in the class too. Initially, they used the time to complete observations, although I also tried to be proactive throughout the day and suggested they complete some in different situations. Having this protected time meant that the observations, and later sessions, were able to happen regularly. This meant that they were able to spend a longer period of time getting to know the learner, which had a positive impact on their interactions.

Access to recording

Jacqui and Emily used weekly Progress Tracks to record new developments. They also completed the more extensive Session sheets for any particularly important sessions, including the sessions that were videoed. These sheets offered the opportunity to make reflections on their own practice as well as pupil progress, although initially, like myself, they found it more challenging to do this.

The development of their own technique as practitioners

The process of supporting my mentees to not only develop their technique but more crucially reflect on their interactions, benefited from the following key points:

1 Pausing to allow mentees to self-reflect
2 Tuning-in to their needs by listening and being observant
3 Fine-tuning my responses

Pausing to allow mentees to self-reflect

Kolb (2014) stressed the importance of self-reflection when introducing his experiential learning cycle. This cycle suggests a model of learning that is dependent on repetition of experiences that the learner reflects upon. Boreham (1987) also reiterates the important role of reflection when discussing learning from experience.

It was not enough for my mentees to simply have plenty of experiences, but also for them to have the opportunity to reflect on these experiences. The model also suggests that following reflection, there must then be some form of 'revision of plans' for next time: an active step in deciding what to do differently, or even what to keep the same.

It was important that I allowed this period of self-reflection by pausing and waiting when it came to video analysis.

By allowing for this self-reflection, I avoided being too directive and risking damaging their confidence. However, I had to consider that my mentees would not necessarily be well practiced in reflecting on their techniques. To give them some practice on reflecting and looking

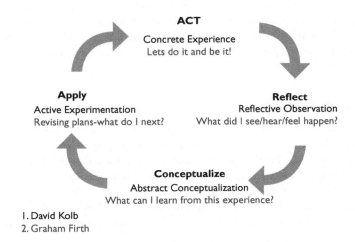

ACT
Concrete Experience
Lets do it and be it!

Apply
Active Experimentation
Revising plans-what do I next?

Reflect
Reflective Observation
What did I see/hear/feel happen?

Conceptualize
Abstract Conceptualization
What can I learn from this experience?

1. David Kolb
2. Graham Firth

Figure 6.2 Experiential Learning Cycles.

for techniques, we watched one of my videos first and I discussed my own reflections as well as asking for theirs.

Tuning-in

In terms of the reflecting part of the cycle, I tried to step back and allow them to lead the discussion where possible. This meant that I needed to listen to how they were feeling through this process, through being observant and effectively 'tuning-in' to each of them. I used the style sheets (see appendix 3) to structure our discussion, referring to them to help with the next part of the cycle: conceptualisation.

Conceptualisation is the area where the greatest amount of direction was needed, especially in the first session. For example, Emily very quickly reflected on her experience by saying 'I know what I was doing wrong, I wasn't waiting for Hayden to finish vocalising before imitating him'. It was important for me to expand on this with her, in order to help to discuss this in terms of conceptualising this. By referring back to the style sheet, I suggested that the technique that she was using in this case was joining-in, rather than imitating. By being more specific about the terminology, Emily would be able to conceptualise this to help her plan for the next time. We also discussed that Hayden actually seemed to be enjoying Emily joining-in with his vocalisations so she wasn't doing something 'wrong'.

The next part of the learning model is what Kolb refers to as 'Active Experimentation' and Firth (2012) usefully uses the question 'What do I do next?' In order to help guide Emily's thoughts on this, I made the suggestion that she focused on tuning-in to Hayden to help her make an informed decision in the future as to whether she joins-in or imitates.

Fine-tuning my response

Emily

From observing Emily's self-critical reflections, I made a conscious decision *not* to over-analyse, or to provide 'constructive/reflective' feedback. Emily was an excellent practitioner, she simply needed help conceptualising her own reflections and for me to ensure she wasn't being overly negative.

Jacqui

Jacqui is an extremely natural practitioner and as such, the focus became giving her the support and theoretical knowledge to better enable her to communicate this and go on to support other

Coordinator Course

Style / Technique List

Video:	
Available look	
Available self / body	
Positioning	
Observes	
Tunes in	
Relaxed	
Enjoyment	
Unhurried	
Does not drive on	
Pauses	
Waits	
Doesn't do too much	
Responsive	
Timing / tempo / pace / flow	
Ways of responding	
Responds to vocalisations	
Responds with running commentary	
Joins in	
Imitates	
Use of touch	
Finds the right moment to develop, build, extend	
Uses scenario 2 when right	
Anything else? Comments	

Figure 6.3 Style sheet.

colleagues. By focussing on discussions of her own and others' videos, I encouraged self-reflection where possible; to enable technical discussion of what made her own interactions flow. I also found a theoretical focus, particularly on parent-infant interaction, meant that Jacqui became a strong voice who provided support to others during larger group discussions.

Reflecting on mentoring

As I reflected on my own practice as a mentor, I realised that it wasn't so much about how their practice changed individually, but what it was that I did as a mentor to enable this change to occur. In terms of the experiential learning cycle, it is key that during the 'acting' and 'reflecting' parts it is important to pause, to give the mentees the opportunity to self-reflect, both at the time of the interaction and during video analysis. It is then during the conceptualisation and application parts of the cycle where more direction is often needed, to help structure their reflections and form a definitive plan for the next session.

Organisational change

One of the more challenging aspects of being a Co-ordinator was beginning to make organisational changes in order to enable more pupils to benefit from Intensive Interaction.

The situation so far

The special school where I work caters for around one hundred pupils, most of whom have a diagnosis of autism. There is a huge range of abilities within the school, but most pupils have some difficulty with social communication, making Intensive Interaction essential. I was lucky to work alongside another Co-ordinator, Jade.

Most staff had some awareness that Intensive Interaction existed, and quite a few had taken part in a twenty-minute introduction session. Some staff also took part in weekly Intensive Interaction sessions in our swimming pool, where they would participate with pupils from their class group. However, Jade and I wanted to integrate sessions more fully into daily school life. In terms of school documentation we had Touch, Physical Contact and Intensive Interaction policies, but often staff were unaware that these existed.

I identified the following barriers to successful implementation of Intensive Interaction:

* Misguided perceptions of Intensive Interaction: frequently including an overemphasis on copying as a technique as well as a lack of understanding of the purpose or outcomes;
* Some staff were unaware of Intensive Interaction: they were often natural practitioners, but were unable to recognise the value of what they were doing so were often not acknowledging or recording progress;
* Antagonists: a few members of staff who would damage the confidence of practitioners within school by belittling the importance of Intensive Interaction. Sometimes these were people who subscribed to the 'We've Always Done It This Way' view (Parsley and Corrigan, 1999), but also included people who had a misguided perception of how Intensive Interaction should be implemented.

It was important to recognise that there was a general acceptance and recognition of Intensive Interaction and that there were lots of enthusiastic people who were prepared to learn. However, there was a risk that due to the barriers, enthusiastic staff members would be discouraged, good practice would go unacknowledged and some staff would continue to hold misguided views about practice and outcomes. As a result, I realised that the following changes were important to give staff the confidence to be able to discuss, practise and record Intensive Interaction:

1   Create a positive and informed culture around Intensive Interaction
   • Stop 'fighting' negativity
   • 'Casual' mentoring
   • Formal small group training
   • Regular opportunities for Intensive Interaction
2   Improve documentation of Intensive Interaction and raise awareness of it
   • Enable staff to document pupil progress
   • Raise awareness of the Touch Policy through training and updates to include the negative consequences of not using touch

Creating positivity about Intensive Interaction

It was important to not only create a positive culture about Intensive Interaction, but also an informed one, with staff who were 'armed' with theoretical knowledge as well as practical experience. The aim was that staff would be confident and able to discuss Intensive Interaction openly.

Don't let the antagonists get you down (stop 'fighting' negativity)

Pratt (1980) recognises that there are usually five categories of individuals in organisations: enthusiasts, supporters, acquiescers, laggards and antagonists. I could certainly recognise individuals from each of these groups within the school and I initially felt myself being drawn to 'fighting' the antagonists. Although it is important to give consideration to each of these groups, the amount of time and resources that I personally had available certainly impacted on this. I soon felt disheartened by my focus on 'battling' against negativity and realised that this was not going to be effective in making long-term changes. Mentoring had given me such a positive experience, creating a sort of ripple effect as more people became engaged with it. This led me to change my focus to creating positivity with the enthusiasts and supporters rather than fighting individual battles against antagonists.

Casual mentoring

By creating a positive impact with my mentees, it created a sense of togetherness: other staff wanted to become involved and I held another set of training sessions to include them. I deliberately kept the training sessions informal, incorporating basic theory with plenty of videos and time for group discussion. This informal style allowed me to get a feel for the mind-set of my colleagues, and particularly any concerns about implementation.

This additional group involved staff from not only my class team, but also another class where I was working at the time.

I found that following our informal training sessions, staff seemed quite inspired to run with their own practice; more importantly, seeming more confident in discussing Intensive Interaction and acknowledging its importance. I also ensured they had access to recording sheets for the pupils in their class.

This led to a lot more positivity around Intensive Interaction: staff would even come up to me through the school day to tell me about some of the successful sessions they had with their pupils.

As a result of this success, Jade and I plan to continue mentoring individuals from key classes across the school to continue to cultivate this positive environment.

Formal group training

Although some staff were aware of Intensive Interaction, there was often a lack of knowledge. Sometimes this was about the range of techniques used: staff often believed you simply had to copy the pupils exactly; but also around the outcomes: some staff believed the aim was to get pupils to copy them eventually.

Therefore, I acknowledged the need for a more formal training programme in addition to mentoring individuals. The mentoring and informal training sessions had all taken place in our own, unpaid time and as happy as we were to do this, I felt it was important for the school to acknowledge the need to schedule such essential training in paid meeting time. This was important to prevent Intensive Interaction from being seen as an optional extra.

Through liaising with the deputy head teacher, I arranged an initial training session with a group of twelve colleagues to be held in staff meeting time. By choosing mainly these supporters and enthusiasts to form this group, we were able to have a vibrant and stimulating training session with plenty of positive contributions from staff members. I also ensured Jacqui was present in the training session and she was able to confidently add to the discussions. This session was hugely successful in terms of creating positivity about Intensive Interaction, with several members of staff going out of their way the following day to express their enjoyment of the session, with some showing interest in completing further training.

Following on from this success, Jade and I held successful discussions with our Senior Leadership Team to arrange training for all staff, again during meeting time.

Regularly scheduled II time

Nind and Hewett (2006) recognise the importance of allowing for 'quality Intensive Interaction time'. One of the biggest developments with my class was the introduction of a daily slot for Intensive Interaction integrated into the timetable. This involved me working closely with the class teacher, who fully supported and recognised the need for Intensive Interaction to be seen as a priority.

This was dedicated time where there was no other focus for our pupils or staff: an opportunity for staff to hone their skills, but also for pupils to have the opportunity to interact without demands being placed. We would split the class group and use a sensory room during this time Fundamentally, the pupils led the session, including if they preferred not to interact, or preferred to interact elsewhere. This led to a greater awareness among staff as it formed part of the school day.

It also meant that we enabled a greater number of repetitions of sessions, which is a crucial element for progress to occur within a process-central model (Hewett, 2012a). As the sessions were occurring so regularly, this meant that pupils, who had previously not seemed to show progress, began to make rapid developments. It meant that we could build on existing successful relationships and expand this to working with other staff. This allowed staff to see positive results as well as having the opportunity to regularly practice their skills and techniques.

Documentation

Recording progress

Now that Intensive Interaction was happening more often, it became more important for progress to be recorded. Previously, staff had not had access to recording, but Jade and I began to introduce recording sheets into classes.

Initially, staff seemed motivated to complete session sheets particularly if they were allocated a key pupil to work with. However, this became more difficult as staffing levels changed. Staff members often felt overwhelmed by the amount of paperwork needed in school, and Intensive Interaction was still viewed as an optional extra. It did seem that if a member of staff was motivated and felt confident in their skills and abilities, they were more likely to record sessions. It is therefore an aspect that I expect to improve over a period of time as more staff are trained and mentored within school.

Still afraid to touch? When documentation isn't enough

By keeping a relaxed and open element to group discussions, staff were able to be honest about some of the issues they felt would prevent Intensive Interaction from happening. One of the biggest revelations was the lack of confidence around issues of touch. There were so many comments about other members of staff being defensive about touch, often citing issues of age-appropriateness. More worryingly, some staff felt that even though they knew the relevant policies were in place, they still felt that the behaviour of other people would prevent them from acting in line with the policies.

This led to a greater amount of time discussing issues of touch and age-appropriateness within the training session. Previously, with the informal training groups, we had only briefly discussed touch as the staff members had seemed confident in using touch and had dismissed issues of age-appropriateness in favour of developmental appropriateness. However, the degree to which other staff felt unable to use touch or even engage a pupil in developmentally appropriate activities was concerning. Hewett (2012b) discusses the negative consequences of treating a person only in line with their chronological age and that effectively this is refusing to acknowledge the inner person. Recognition of the importance of this led me to reassess the need for further attention in this area.

This also reiterates the importance of focussing on enthusiasts not antagonists. Out of the group of people I trained, not one felt that touch itself was inappropriate, but rather that other people (antagonists) would make them feel that they would be judged for being unprofessional. The important issue here is to try and give the enthusiasts and supporters confidence and importantly, information so that they are able to openly discuss the reasons for touch, rather than withholding it.

Acknowledging success

In terms of evaluating success, I find it helpful to remember that although my goal is to make widespread organisational change, it is also important to remember each individual pupil as a person. Intensive Interaction changes the world for each person and this is a rightly significant achievement. This is not to dismiss widespread organisational change; in fact, it is this that motivates it but it serves to remind us to be mindful of this and celebrate each person's journey.

References

Boreham, N.C. (1987) Learning from experience in diagnostic problem solving. In: Eysenck, M.W., Richardson, J.T.E. and Piper, D.W. (ed.). *Student Learning: Research in Education and Cognitive Psychology*. Milton Keynes, UK Society for Research into Higher Education & Open University Press.

Bowlby, J. (1953) Some causes of mental ill-health. In Bowlby, J. (1953) *Child Care and the Growth of Love*. London: Pelican.

Firth, G., Berry, R. and Irvine, C. (2010) *Understanding Intensive Interaction Contexts and Concepts for Professionals and Families*. London, UK: Jessica Kingsley Publishers.

Hewett, D. (2012a) What is intensive interaction? Curriculum, process, and approach. In Hewett, D. (ed.). *Intensive Interaction. Theoretical Perspectives*. London, UK: SAGE Publications. pp. 137–154.

Hewett, D. (2012b) Some Associated Issues and Topics. In Hewett, D., Barber, M., Firth, G., Harrison, T. (ed.). *The Intensive Interaction Handbook*. London, UK: SAGE Publications. pp. 133–141.

Hewett, D. (2013) Intensive Interaction and people with autism and complex needs. Paper/workshop presented to the National Autistic Society Conference, Autism & Complex Needs, Birmingham, 15th October 2016.

Kellett, M., Nind, M. and Mary, K. (2003) *Implementing Intensive Interaction in Schools: Guidance for Practitioners, Managers and Co-ordinators*. London, UK: David Fulton Publishers.

Kolb, D.A. (2014) *Experiential Learning: Experience as the Source of Learning and Development*. Upper Saddle River, NJ: Pearson FT Press.

Lamb, M.E., Bornstein, M.H. & Teti, D.M. (2002) *Development in Infancy*. New Jersey: Lawrence Erlbaum.

Meltzoff, A. (1999) Born to Learn: What infants learn from watching Us. In: Fox, N.A., Leavitt, L.A. and Warhol, J.G. (ed.). *The Role of Early Experience in Infant Development*. St Louis, MO: Johnson & Johnson Pediatric Institute.

Nind, M. and Hewett, D. (2006) *Access to Communication: Developing the Basics of Communication with People with Severe Learning Difficulties Through Intensive Interaction*. 2nd edn. London, UK: David Fulton Publishers.

Parsley, K. and Corrigan, P. (1999) *Quality Improvement in Health Care: Putting Evidence into Practice*. 2nd edn. Cheltenham, UK: Stanley Thornes Publishers.

Pratt, D. (1980) *Curriculum Design and Development*. New York, NY: Harcourt Brace Jovanovich. p.112–113.

Schore, A.N. (2003) The Human Unconscious: The development of the right brain and its role in early emotional life. In: Greene, V. (ed) *Emotional Development in Psychoanalysis, attachment theory and neuroscience: creating connections*. Brighton & NY: Routledge.

Chapter 7

Intensive Interaction mentoring process and the use of video

Kaisa Martikainen

This chapter gives an invaluable understanding of the crucial importance of using video in mentoring. Kaisa describes in detail the process of shooting videos, choosing a successful video clip to be reviewed with her mentee and the principles of empowering discussions in mentor and practitioner meetings. Informed by Video Interaction Guidance (VIG), Kaisa's sensitive and empowering mentoring style is illustrated with transcripts of conversations she had with her mentees. Kaisa also describes the practitioner's experiences in using Intensive Interaction with a person with complex communication needs as well as her experiences and insights on the mentoring process.

Introduction

Intensive Interaction is a practical approach to interacting with people with learning disabilities and/or autism who do not find it easy communicating or being social. The approach focusses on developing the 'fundamentals of communication' (see appendix 1) – the communication concepts and performances that basically precede speech development: enjoying being with another person, developing the ability to attend, concentrating and being attentive, learning to do sequences of activity with another person, taking turns, sharing personal space, using and understanding eye contacts, facial expressions, physical contacts, nonverbal communication, using vocalisations with meaning and learning to regulate and control arousal levels (Nind and Hewett, 2006). These fundamentals are based on similar developmental processes that babies go through with their carers during the first and second year of their lives.

When we adopt Intensive Interaction as an approach we adopt a particular interactive style. In our interactions with our communication partners we use Intensive Interaction techniques: an available look and body position, tuning in and observing, a relaxed style and observable enjoyment. We are unhurried and don't drive on, we wait and use pauses, we don't do too much, we join in and are responsive in many ways to the other person. And finally, we find the right moment to develop, build and extend (Hewett, 2012). Intensive Interaction sessions should always be playful and enjoyable for both partners.

Shooting videos is an essential tool in Intensive Interaction. Practitioners are recommended to collect videos of interactions with each learner on a weekly basis (Barber, 2012b). The main purpose of collecting video evidence of interactions is to use it to assist in the recognition of progress over time. The videos also enable practitioners to draw from their own experiences: learning what works and what does not, what types of responses are likely to keep the learner interested and potentially encourage them to explore the situation further (Barber, 2012a).

Practitioners may develop their interactive style either by reflecting on their own interaction or through guided reflection with a mentor. A mentor is a person who has more knowledge and experience in Intensive Interaction.

Video-based mentoring

As a mentor, I have used videos to support practitioners to develop their interaction skills with people with complex communication needs. My mentoring style is a combination of principles taken from Intensive Interaction, Video Interaction Guidance (VIG); (Kennedy, Landor and Todd, 2011), Video Enhanced Reflective Practice (VERP); (Kennedy, Landor and Todd, 2015) and OIVA Interaction Model (Onnistutaan [succeed] Innostutaan [get inspired], Videon Avulla [by using video]) (Burakoff and Martikainen, 2015).

VIG, VERP and OIVA are reflective practices enhanced by the use of video. They aim at improving effective communication in naturally occurring situations, and involve video recordings of real-life situations, followed by a shared review of the edited clips in small group meetings with a guide. They are strengths-based and empowerment-based approaches to skills in communication, reflection and critical analysis, and are founded on the belief that a successful interaction requires a sensitive partnership. A sensitive interaction style has been highlighted in the literature as one of the most important factors supporting communication between people with complex communication needs and learning difficulties and their communication partners (see, for example, Nafstad and Rødbroe, 1999; Nind and Hewett, 2006; Zeedyk, 2008).

The guide or mentor works with the practitioners in a way that allows them space to reflect on interactions together and discover for themselves what kind of practical actions are needed to develop their interactions. The guidance is delivered through a dialogical, cooperative relationship. The focus of the video-based guidance is on reviewing successful moments of interaction and seeking out elements that support sensitive partnership.

In VIG, VERP and OIVA, video is also used to support the mentor's own skills in guiding mentees (Kennedy and Landor, 2015). They film themselves occasionally during their meetings with mentees for video-based reflection. This enables the mentors to learn from their own experiences: the focus in watching the videos is to recognise the successful moments in guiding, and the moments where the mentee's needs are met sensitively.

Core elements of mentoring

My mentoring style is strengths-based and empowerment-based and founded on the belief that successful interaction requires sensitive partnership. The aim is to improve effective communication in naturally occurring situations.

Mentoring is based on the following core elements: video recording of Intensive Interaction in real-life situations, using edited clips of the video for shared review and discussion with the practitioner, highlighting moments of successful use of the interactive style of Intensive Interaction, adopting a non-blaming approach and widening the focus on competencies, and being willing to understand things from new perspectives (Silhanova and Sancho, 2011). The core of the relationship's dynamic between mentor and mentee is to achieve mutual understanding. This mutual understanding is activated through dialogue, which is the main tool to support learning and reflection.

Video recording Intensive Interaction in naturalistic situations

During an Intensive Interaction project with a particular individual, I have regular meetings with the person and the staff working with them in their own surroundings (group home, day activity centre, school, etc.). From the very start my aim is to support staff to become confident and skilful practitioners, able to implement Intensive Interaction through their everyday practice with the people they support. Before starting the practical work, one or two members of staff are chosen as main practitioners for that person. Their role also means they have responsibilities in involving and mentoring the other members of the team.

My visits are usually structured in a particular way. First, I have an Intensive Interaction session with the person, which is videoed by a member of staff, whenever possible. Then, the roles are switched, and the member of staff becomes the practitioner and I video their session with the person. These meetings usually end with a short discussion about how the session went for both of us.

Using edited clips for shared review

Regular meetings with the whole staff team as well as the main practitioners working with the individual is key to the mentoring process. In these meetings, we watch short video clips I have selected from Intensive Interaction videos previously shot with the person. Whilst it is important that I show videos of myself working with the person, I focus more on the staff's practice in order to develop their skills and confidence. The video clips I choose show the best possible examples of interaction between the two people, the exceptional and the model for future development and change (Kennedy and Landor, 2015). The point is that the model is provided from the practitioner's own repertoire of behaviours, so it is within their capacity and experience. In those meetings the practitioner and the rest of the team see and discuss how to best achieve successful interactions with a particular individual, and how to steer the situation in a positive direction at points when the interaction is at risk of failing.

Highlighting successful moments of Intensive Interaction

Although a practitioner's practice may be very good, they may have difficulties in explaining why the interaction was successful (Jarvis and Lyon, 2015). The mentor's role is to guide practitioners to see the effects of their successful use of Intensive Interaction techniques, and to help them recognise their strengths and feel relaxed.

The following extract – Extract 1 – is a transcript of a videoed dialogue I had with a mentee, at the end of our mentoring session. In this extract, Paula is the Intensive Interaction practitioner, Kaisa the mentor and Tina a person with complex communication needs. Before this dialogue Kaisa and Paula have watched a 1 minute and 40 second video of Paula and Tina's Intensive Interaction session.

Extract 1

KAISA: We have discussed the II techniques of a practitioner and how important they are in creating communicative moments. What do you think after watching this video, what makes you especially happy?
(Kaisa watches a still image of a successful moment in the video, then looks at Paula, smiles, and turns back to the still image.)
(Kaisa and Paula watch the still image.)
KAISA: If you think about these.
(Kaisa watches and points at a paper where practitioner's II techniques are written, turns and looks at Paula.)

PAULA: Mmm.
(Paula watches the still image and then looks at the paper with the II techniques.)
PAULA: I'm happy that in the video the activity is relaxed and unhurried. (Paula looks at the paper again. Kaisa looks at Paula and nods.)
(Paula watches the still image.)
PAULA: It's my active searching of eye contact and getting the eye contact.
(Paula watches the still image and looks at Kaisa.)
PAULA: But also, even though Tina sometimes turns away she always comes back and re-establishes eye contact again.
KAISA: Mmmm.
(Kaisa looks at Paula and nods.)
(Paula points at the still image with her finger. Kaisa watches the still image.)
PAULA: Several times.
KAISA: Mmm.
KAISA: How do you make that happen?
(Kaisa rises, looks at Paula and smiles.)

In video-based guidance the use of video clips and still images have an important role in discussion. The mentor uses the footage as an object of shared interest whilst building a strong attuned interaction with the mentee (Kennedy, 2011). In this extract, we see how the focus varies back and forth from the eye contacts between practitioner (Paula) and mentor (Kaisa), to the sheet of paper with the Intensive Interaction techniques written, and to the still image on the screen. At the beginning of the dialogue (lines 1– 4), the practitioner needs time to process what she has just watched to be able to reply to her mentor. The questions the mentor asks are based on the video and allow the practitioner to analyse her own practice, and understand her technique. It is important that the mentor keeps a balance between allowing the mentee to reflect on their own practice by themselves, and providing them with some support (Kennedy and Landor, 2015).

Widening the focus on competencies and being willing to understand things from a new perspective

In the shared review, the mentor and practitioner co-create 'reality' through their conversations (Silhanova and Sancho, 2011). Instead of being an expert, the mentor is a 'collaborative explorer' co-creating meanings with the practitioner. In other words, the practitioner's ideas affect the mentor and vice versa. The main focus is to explore daily interactions, and how the practitioner then develops her practice to understanding Intensive Interaction on a deeper level and in a wider range of contexts.

The following extract shows how the dialogue between mentor and practitioner helps the practitioner to widen her insights and her understanding. This dialogue is an extension to the first dialogue, described in Extract 1. In this extract, again, Paula is the Intensive Interaction practitioner, Kaisa the mentor, and Tina the person with complex communication needs. Prior to having this discussion, Kaisa and Paula watched in detail some shorter clips of the longer 1 minute and 40 seconds' video of Paula and Tina's Intensive Interaction session.

Extract 2

PAULA: I think I talk to her all the time.
(Paula watches a still image of a successful moment of the video.)

KAISA: I think so yes.
> (Kaisa looks at Paula.)

PAULA: I'm not sure about the meaning of what I am saying, but I usually talk to Tina when I'm with her..
> (Paula and Kaisa look at each other.)

KAISA: Yes. What do you think? Why is that?
> (Kaisa points at a piece of paper where the II techniques are written. Paula looks at the paper.)

PAULA: Maybe this is just my way of letting her know I'm there for her, and that I am interested.
> (Paula watches the piece of paper with II techniques and turns to Kaisa.)

KAISA: Yes.
> (Kaisa looks at Paula.)

PAULA: I have noticed that I ask her questions, even though I know I'm not going to get any verbal answers.
> (Paula and Kaisa look at each other.)

KAISA: Yes, you get her responses through her body language though.
> (Kaisa looks at Paula, nods and smiles.)

PAULA: Yes.
> (Paula looks at the paper with the II techniques.)

KAISA: I also think that you have a tender tone in your voice when you speak.
> (Kaisa watches the still image, turns to Paula and smiles.)

PAULA: Mmm.

KAISA: I also think that it helps Tina to keep focussed.
> (Kaisa looks at Paula and smiles.)

PAULA: Yes. And maybe Tina has become more familiar with this. And since she recognises my voice, it is a lot easier to get this kind of interaction again and again. She is good at recognising voices and she is sensitive to the way I speak to her. All of us have our own style. I notice that Tina recognises my style.
> (Kaisa and Paula look at each other and smile.)

KAISA: Yes, yes.
> (Kaisa looks at Paula and smiles.)

In this extract, Paula wants to discuss the amount of speech she is using when interacting with a person who cannot answer her with spoken words. In this video, her style is very sensitive but she is not aware of it. She uses verbal and vocal communicative responses similar to those of 'motherese', the communicative style of sensitive mothers with their babies (Paavola, 2006). After listening to the practitioner's point of view, the mentor (Kaisa) responds by commenting on the effects of using motherese with Tina (lines 9, 11 and 13). This conversation helps the practitioner to understand and describe the situation as well as her ideas from a different perspective (line 14).

Adopting a non-blaming approach

It is important that the mentor creates an encouraging, enjoyable and safe atmosphere for the mentee (Kennedy and Landor, 2015; Doria, Strathie and Strathie, 2011). Rather than focusing on what is not working, the mentor compliments the practitioner on what she does well. This asserts to the practitioner that the mentor can recognize her strengths and the mentee feels reassured and supported to bring positive change to her practice.

Extract 3 gives an example of how to bring the mentee to reflect on less positive aspects of their practice and help them change their perspective by themselves. This dialogue follows on from the dialogues described in extracts 1 and 2. In this extract again, Paula is the Intensive Interaction practitioner, Kaisa the mentor, and Tina a person with complex communication needs. Before this dialogue, Kaisa and Paula have watched in detail some shorter clips of the longer 1 minute and 40 second video of Paula and Tina's Intensive Interaction session.

Extract 3

KAISA: What are your thoughts about the video we just watched together. I'm thinking about what you've said … that Tina has been different lately.
(Kaisa looks at Paula, nods and smiles.)

PAULA: Yes … or the last few days have been different.
(Kaisa and Paula look each other.)

KAISA: Mmm.
(Kaisa looks at Paula. Paula watches a still image of a successful moment in the video.)

PAULA: Our interaction hasn't been like the interaction we are looking at. We have had some interactions, but it hasn't been like that.
(Paula watches the still image.)

KAISA: Mmm.

PAULA: I think so.

KAISA: Mmm.
(Kaisa looks at Paula.)

PAULA: During the last few days. On the other hand I think that I have had many morning shifts, and in the morning there are not many possibilities to interact because she always leaves to go to the day activity centre. So there is no time.
(Paula watches the still image and turns to Kaisa. Kaisa and Paula look at each other.)

KAISA: Mmm.

PAULA: No possibilities to recreate situations like this. Anything like this.
(Paula and Kaisa watch the still image in the video.)

KAISA: Yes, you mean that you have to hurry.
(Kaisa looks at Paula.)

PAULA: Maybe so. When I start to think about it … it might be that. (Paula looks at Kaisa.)

KAISA: Mmm.

PAULA: The reason.
(Kaisa and Paula watch the still image.)

KAISA: What are your thoughts on this?
(Kaisa and Paula watch the still image.)

KAISA: Do you see something in the video that you could take away with you, and apply to your daily routines? When do you next meet Tina?
(Kaisa and Paula look at each other.)

PAULA: I think the point is that I must ensure there are moments like this. That's it I think.
(Paula looks at Kaisa and smiles.)

KAISA: Yes.
(Kaisa looks at Paula and smiles.)
(Paula watches the still image.)

PAULA: I need to ensure that there is time to create moments like this one throughout my shift.
(Paula looks at Kaisa.)

KAISA: Yes.
    (Kaisa looks at Paula.)
PAULA: I am sure that's what it is.
KAISA: Yes.
    (Kaisa and Paula look at each other and smile.)

On the one hand, the mentor's aim here is to help the practitioner express her thoughts and feelings about this less successful interaction (line 1). On the other hand, the mentor's role is to help the practitioner to realise that she has the skills and the sensitivity to create successful moments of Intensive Interaction with the person (lines 18 and 19). By bringing the practitioner to reflect on what she thinks and what really takes place in the interaction, the mentor helps the practitioner to think about concrete things she can do for successful interactions and positive change.

Practitioner's insights on Intensive Interaction

Towards the end of this Intensive Interaction project, I had a meeting with Paula. At the beginning of our meeting, we watched two video clips: the first one was a baseline video of Paula and Tina, and the second video clip was both of them again, but shot ten months later.

In our meeting, Paula tells that she sees a big change in her own interactive style with Tina. She explains how useful it has been to watch videos of her own practice and see herself change and become a confident practitioner:

> *It makes me feel good to see the change. I clearly didn't know how to interact with a person with complex communication needs in the first video. It is so important for me that we have shot these videos. I can now see how things have really happened.*

She spoke about the hurry and the many things staff have in mind. However, she feels happy that she has found time to do Intensive Interaction, and she recognises how valuable and significant these moments are to the person she is interacting with:

> *Sometimes I feel like a steam train. I am in a hurry and I have many things in my mind at the same time. Nonetheless I manage to find moments to be present and concentrate on an interaction like we have seen in the videos. I can see how Tina enjoys these moments. It is important that we have Intensive Interaction sessions.*

What is more, she expressed that through Intensive Interaction she has learnt to focus on the moment. She used to always have a goal for her interactions. She has now realised how important it is to approach a situation with an open mind, and to observe how the other person feels, and what she or her brings to the interaction and respond accordingly:

> *I feel that I have learnt to be present and to live in the moment. It was a natural way for me to always have a goal before. But in an Intensive Interaction moment, the only goal is to be present and see what is going to happen.*

Paula summarised the importance of Intensive Interaction to all professionals working with people with complex communication needs:

I think that knowing Intensive Interaction is necessary for all professionals who work with people with severe learning disabilities and autism. It is important to take time to think about social interaction. There are many other aspects of the job, such as nursing issues, etc. It is essential that professionals don't forget the importance of interacting with the people they are supporting. It is necessary for well-being. It is not enough if you get food and clean clothes. Everyone has a right to interact.

My aim from the beginning of our Intensive Interaction period together was to empower this practitioner to find courage and skills to do Intensive Interaction herself on a daily basis.

I met Paula six months after the meeting and asked her about her interactions in the group home. She told me that Tina is happy. They have regular Intensive Interaction moments together. Sometimes these moments are planned but mostly they occur spontaneously. Paula told me that she often realises afterwards that a lot of their interaction is actually Intensive Interaction.

There has been an important turnover of staff at Tina's group home. However, Paula said she made sure the new staff are briefed about the use of Intensive Interaction with Tina, and ensures they all watch the videos.

References

Barber, M. (2012a) Promoting Communication rather than Generating Data. In Hewett, D. ed., *Intensive Interaction Theoretical Perspectives,* 1st edn. London, UK: SAGE Publications, pp. 88–103.

Barber, M. (2012b) Recording the Activities and Maintaining the Processes. In Hewett, D., Firth, G., Barber, M., and Harrison, T., eds., *The Intensive Interaction Handbook*. London, UK: SAGE Publications, pp. 90–114.

Burakoff, K. and Martikainen, K. (2015) OIVA – Supporting Staff for Better Interaction with People with Complex Communication Needs. In Kennedy, H., Landor, M., and Todd, L., eds., *Video Enhanced Reflective Practice. Professional Development through Attuned Interactions.* London, UK: Jessica Kingsley Publishers, pp. 136–146.

Doria, M., Strathie, C. and Strathie, S. (2011) Supporting Vulnerable Families to Change through VIG. In Kennedy, H., Landor, M., and Todd, L., eds., *Video Interaction Guidance. A Relationship-Based Intervention to Promote Attunement, Empathy and Wellbeing.* London, UK: Jessica Kingsley Publishers, pp. 121–133.

Hewett, D. (2012) Preparing for Intensive Interaction. In Hewett, D., Firth, G., Barber, M., and Harrison, T., *The Intensive Interaction Handbook*. London, UK: SAGE Publications, pp. 29–44.

Jarvis, J. and Lyon, S. (2015) What makes Video Enhanced Reflective Practice (VERP) Successful for System Change? In Kennedy, H., Landor, M., and Todd, L., eds., *Video Enhanced Reflective Practice. Professional Development through Attuned Interactions.* London, UK: Jessica Kingsley Publishers, pp. 35–46.

Kennedy, H. (2011) What is Video Interaction Guidance (VIG)? In Kennedy, H., Landor, M., and Todd, L., eds., *Video Interaction Guidance. A Relationship-Based Intervention to Promote Attunement, Empathy and Wellbeing.* London, UK: Jessica Kingsley Publishers, pp. 20–42.

Kennedy, H. and Landor, M. (2015) Introduction. In Kennedy, H., Landor, M., and Todd, L., eds., *Video Enhanced Reflective Practice. Professional Development through Attuned Interactions.* London, UK: Jessica Kingsley Publishers, pp. 18–34.

Kennedy, H., Landor, M. and Todd, L., eds. (2011) *Video Interaction Guidance. A Relationship-Based Intervention to Promote Attunement, Empathy and Wellbeing.* London, UK: Jessica Kingsley Publishers.

Kennedy, H., Landor, M. and Todd, L., eds. (2015) *Video Enhanced Reflective Practice. Professional Development through Attuned Interactions.* London, UK: Jessica Kingsley Publishers.

Nafstad, A. and Rødbroe, I. (1999) *Co-creating communication. Perspectives on Diagnostic Education for Individuals Who Are Congenitally Deafblind and Individuals Whose Impairments May Have Similar Effects.* Dronninglund, Denmark: Nord-Press.

Nind, M. and Hewett, D. (2006) *Access to Communication: Developing the Basics of Communication with People with Severe Learning Difficulties through Intensive Interaction.* 2nd edn. London, UK: David Fulton Publishers.

Paavola, L. (2006) *Maternal sensitive responsiveness, characteristics and relations to child early communicative and linguistic development.* PhD. Acta Universitatis Ouluensis B 73. Available at: http://jultika.oulu.fi/files/isbn9514282035.pdf [Accessed 5 Apr. 2016].

Silhanova, K. and Sancho, M. (2011) VIG and the Supervision Process. In Kennedy, H., Landor, M., and Todd, L., eds., *Video Interaction Guidance. A Relationship-Based Intervention to Promote Attunement, Empathy and Wellbeing.* London, UK: Jessica Kingsley Publishers, pp. 43–57.

Zeedyk, M. S., ed. (2008) *Promoting Social Interaction for Individuals with Communicative Impairments: Making Contact.* London, UK: Jessica Kingsley Publishers.

Chapter 8

Managing a service that specialises in Intensive Interaction provision

A discussion between Cath Brockie and Jules McKim, co-editor

Cath Brockie

Cath gives an account of how to successfully embed Intensive Interaction into a service's values and ethics. She recounts her journey with John, an adult with severe learning disabilities and behaviours that services found challenging and how Intensive Interaction changed his life. As CEO of her provider organisation she explains how Intensive Interaction has become the core of her service's DNA.

Please introduce yourself and Corran's services

My name is Cath Brockie and I've been the owner and manager of support services for people with a range of complex needs and specifically communication difficulties for over 20 years. We support people with learning disabilities, mental health needs, dementia and acquired brain injuries. Corran Dean is our new site in Worcestershire, England. This came off the back of Corran Vale, the original business in Wales, which is still running. That is where I started practicing Intensive Interaction (II) and I have carried it on into the services in England. We provide residential services – 24/7, 52 weeks a year, with high levels of support for people with very complex needs; short breaks and day opportunities across both sites.

What is your background?

In some ways my background goes right back to childhood. I was classified as 'complex needs' when I was a child myself and would almost certainly have been diagnosed as being on the autistic spectrum had I not had a mother who really didn't believe in 'labelling'. I had additional needs that meant I was supported differently at school, so I think I have always had empathy for the people I work with and have some understanding of their difficulties.

I began my work in special needs teaching. I feel I had always been practicing Intensive Interaction though I didn't know that was what it was. I used my non-verbal communication, my facial expressions, gave people time to process but I didn't give it that technical term. I discovered Intensive Interaction when I later worked for the NHS in Wales. I worked within the psychology-led team of the Challenging Behaviour service. I was lucky enough to get funding to attend a Phoebe Caldwell course. That was where my formal learning and understanding of Intensive Interaction began. I started training my own staff team in Intensive Interaction using Phoebe Caldwell's DVDs. We didn't use II much back then, it didn't underpin our services in the way it does now. So, although I built it into the staff induction and we talked about doing it, we didn't really do it. It kind of floated around for some years.

It was not until I met Dave Hewett at a conference and got one of his DVDs that I felt the staff team would connect better with the footage included. Also I felt that Dave's literature and handbooks were really helpful for me and my staff to know what I was doing and why I was doing it. For example, when I had done II training previously I had never been made aware of the 'fundamentals of communication' (FOC) (Nind & Hewett, 2001 – see appendix 1). So, Dave's work really brought me on, and that was when I really took a hold of II and embraced it. I realised that this was what we should be doing with the people we support.

How did you come to be on the Co-ordinator Course?

I got to the point with some of the staff that I was trying to mentor where I didn't know how to move them on. We were 'stuck' with aspects of II and we weren't getting the results that we knew we could with the approach. I was able to have really good interactions with John at the time and yet the other members of staff couldn't. I couldn't understand what the problem was, what the difference was between my approach and theirs. I had moved to England and was living fairly close to Dave, so I asked if I could come round and show him the videos we had made of myself and the other staff. Straight away Dave was able to give me some really useful analysis of these videos and he recommended that I attend the Co-ordinator Course, which would show me how to move the staff team forward with their II.

What is the current use of II within Corran's services?

We had only been using II with one service user, John. We hadn't fully understood or seen the benefits of using II with other people. I was intuitively using it with John. I had a very intense relationship with this guy because of the number of years I had lived with him. The staff were struggling with using II themselves: there was some resistance too at times. They also saw when I was interacting with John, he would light up and we would have these beautiful non-verbal conversations and it made them feel inadequate because they weren't able to get that same response. People referred to it as 'magic' and felt it was a result of a 'special' relationship I had with John. I think it takes a few years to truly get to grips with the practice of II and to be able to switch your skill sets and adapt to each individual you are working with. I had been doing this with John and I had many more opportunities to work with John as I was living with him.

Some staff would say they were going to do it and then when I came back to ask where the video footage was it had mysteriously disappeared. On other occasions, the recording sheets had not been filled in, or they had actually been playing games with toys when they thought they had been doing II. Clearly, they didn't fully comprehend what they were being asked to do and the reasons for it.

What were your expectations of the course for yourself and your staff?

My main aim was to be able to develop the skills to be able to teach Intensive Interaction to my staff team. Also, underpinning this, was to develop my understanding and ability to express the rationale for II. Previously, if staff asked me why we were doing II my reply would have been, 'It's because I've asked you!' I didn't really know enough about it. I hadn't come across the 'fundamentals of communication' before. I wanted to be able to stand there confidently and be able to explain the rationale.

Who was your case study person?

John – my diamond, a one-off who taught me everything I know. I think he really brought on my II practice because he wasn't easy. He wouldn't be someone you would pick to do II with if you wanted an easy ride. Using II with John was complicated, but what made it easier was my close relationship with him.

What was John's history and background?

John had the diagnosis of Down's syndrome with associated severe learning disabilities and autism. Although he never had a formal diagnosis of autism, he was described in his care plan as having 'autistic traits'. John was my original residential service user in Wales. He moved into the service after a very long transition in January 2001. He was born in the 1960s at a time when it was believed autism may have been caused by 'cold parenting'. This may have contributed to the authority's decision to take him away from his family and put him in an asylum. He had been in institutional care since he was 6 years old. John developed very undesirable behaviours as a result of his very negative experiences. He was massively institutionalised and had many negative experiences. As a result, he didn't trust people at all. Human contact was purely for functional reasons, in order to get his basic needs met: food, drink and warmth. He had no real social contact whatsoever as a result of the experiences he had. In my opinion, he had clearly been physically and psychologically abused within the institutions. For the first eight years of his time with me, he lived in my home. I had one or two other support workers who assisted me to give me time off.

With the Care in the Community Act and the closure of the asylums, John was one of the last people to be resettled from the closure of Hensol Castle in Cardiff. They had tried to resettle him a few times previously and each time he had gone back to Hensol under section. When they eventually closed Hensol he had to go for good and he was placed in a house with two other individuals from Hensol. He subsequently ended up in an Assessment and Treatment Unit (ATU) for two years, taking up a wing of the unit, sometimes locked behind double doors, viewed at times through a one-way window. He had very limited interactions with other people and the ones he did have were not very positive. The contact he did have was mainly with males as he was deemed to have not liked females and/or be too challenging for the female staff.

I met John when I was a support worker with the Challenging Behaviour Service with the NHS. I wasn't working directly with him at the time. When I set up a service on my own, I was quickly approached by John's social worker and asked whether I would consider giving John a placement. That's when it all started with John.

He had huge deficits in his communication. He was non-verbal but used sounds, phonics to communicate. His receptive skills were very impaired. You had to understand the context of his sounds to understand the meaning. He used his behaviour to communicate most of the time. His behaviours were his way of saying that he felt frustrated, that he didn't feel loved, that he had no social connection at all with anybody. I think his behaviours were also telling me that he had had a very rough time in life and that he didn't trust anybody. We were starting from ground zero. He used behaviours at times to call out for social attention but also to keep you away. He avoided demand, kept people away, because I suppose then he knew he wouldn't be hurt by them. He was a very fearful, anxious person. When I first got to know him he was on high doses of anti-psychotic medication and had been for many years. He lived in a bit of an anti-psychotic medication 'bubble'. Working with John over the years, and particularly with his communication, we were able to reduce this medication down to very little at the end.

John's behaviours were classified as so 'extremely challenging' that he was funded to live in a house on his own. He was deemed to never be able to have social contact or interaction with people. He had been very self-injurious and had injured others too. He had multiple scars all over his body. He had previously head-butted through double-glazed windows. At one period, he vomited frequently as a result of his high levels of anxiety. When he became anxious, this anxiety could last for seven or eight hours of extreme behaviour. As a result of his behaviours he was kept virtually imprisoned within the ATU.

When you look at his life with us at Corran and what he was able to do as a result of us working with his communication, it is amazing to see the change he went through: John went on foreign holidays, he ate meals every day with other people. When I first met John, you presented him food and then you got out of his room. The whole act of having a meal was hugely distressing for him: the waiting and the anxiety of possible choking. John choked many times as, in the past, he was left on his own during meals. So, there was a lot of anxiety around mealtimes that changed a lot during his time with us at Corran.

When you look at the middle and end of his life, he really was a different person. People who knew John from the unit, would stop us in the street and ask 'Is that John?' and couldn't believe it as he was so calm and relaxed and able to enjoy community visits. He had visitors at home. He had parties at his house and at friend's houses. His world completely changed: he became a social animal, like the rest of us.

Some of this was happening before but it wasn't until after I had started doing the Co-ordinator Course that things started to change pace.

What were your experiences and lessons learned when engaging with John using II?

Although I had been practicing II with John I had never put pen to paper about the sessions. I had never watched my videos back with the style sheet (see appendix 3). So, when with John, in the sessions, I found it useful to have the style sheet out and visibly in front of me to work from. That felt very odd initially. I have a natural tendency to be overly critical of myself, of my own practice. I will rip it to bits and so I was a bit reticent taking the video footage back to the course to show other people. It was amazing what other people saw in my practice that I had missed, particularly the positives. Initially I feel I had a tendency to push away the praise and to say 'no, it needs to be better,' as that's the person I am. I wasn't always happy with it and thought I was missing things.

Unfortunately, as my practice improved, John's health deteriorated. When I look back and see what I later realised would be our last videoed interaction, I see I captured a moment: John was very ill and I was that tuned in through II that John was able to communicate that there was something seriously wrong with him physically. I stopped videoing straight away and immediately phoned the doctor. That was the beginning of the end for John. I don't think I would have noticed this if I hadn't been using II. I had learned not to drive on, to pause and to wait, to tune in to the real subtle exchanges, to slow down to John's pace which had become slower than normal due to his failing health.

Again, this was illustrated both by mine and others' videos: we could all see moments where people weren't tuned in and were distracted as well as moments when they were very absorbed. This all helped to define this essential aspect of the approach. I told myself: practice what you preach and live for the moment. Turn the radio off, leave the mobile phone out of the room, don't have it buzzing in my pocket because it is a distraction that would take me away from every finite second that I had with John. I think I learned to enjoy II more through experiencing more positive sessions and 'getting it': through feeling those 'magic moments' where your heart melts or you want to jump with joy because you've made that human connection. As we were tracking developments and analysing videos systematically, I could see John's confidence with the FOCs developing. All of a sudden, II had a purpose. Although we don't drive on, and don't have an agenda, equally I could see the emergent outcomes happening and it therefore enabled me to focus better on what I was doing at the time and let go of all the other stuff.

John became a much calmer individual. This wasn't to do with his health decline. Although he was becoming more and more unwell he still had the ability to be very challenging. That stayed right to the very end. However, the frequency and intensity was far less. He would only be challenging if he felt that somebody was really not listening to him. He became far more tolerant of people. He was actively seeking out contact with people. When John was first with us and for some years after, he would spend vast amounts of time in his room alone. He would shut himself away unless he wanted to seek you out for food or drink. Towards the end, he was the total opposite – he never wanted to be alone. I managed to secure 2:1 staffing at the end as John was wanting to spend all his time with people. Staff were experiencing challenging behaviour when they tried to leave him alone! That was purely based on the fact that he wanted human interaction all the time, he wanted to be with people. That was the complete opposite of the man I first met. He would initiate contact, he would have two-way exchanges with people. His whole repertoire of communication expanded: we were seeing advances in his communication right up until the day he died.

His health was declining, but his communication was actually developing and we could see this on the videos and track it on the progress sheets. He was tapping on his stomach as a playful, turn taking aspect of his communication. II did also impact and positively affect his functional communication: previously when hungry, John would be challenging. Later he began to lead staff to the kitchen to express hunger. Crucially though, II gave him an outlet for phatic, more commonly known as social chit-chat, and that hugely diminished his frustration. Staff went from complaining that he was being aggressive to complaining that he wanted to spend all his time with them! They were finding it wearing and this was a real issue. John had become quite demanding. It became a different management issue and this led to him having more support. This meant that the interactions could continue while the second member of staff prepared a meal for example – John found kitchen environments stressful. The vomiting stopped completely for some years as a result of improving his communication and giving him a sense of purpose in life.

When I saw the beautiful interactions John and the staff were able to have, particularly in those last 12 months of his life, in some ways I regret not using II to such an extent earlier on. Reducing his behaviours and making him calmer, increasing his sociability to such an extent that he was not wanting to be left at night: all this made a huge difference to his quality of life, until the end of his life. The difference extended to clinical environments. It used to be highly distressing for John to be admitted to hospital. Later, it was an absolute breeze by comparison. I felt previously that I had even, unknowingly, inflicted psychological cruelty on this man through the use of behavioural approaches to modify his challenging behaviour. When he was really challenging, we would be telling him 'No' and giving him time alone, retreating, when probably what he really wanted was contact, was human connection.

After John's death, I began to doubt whether I could practice II with anyone else. Did my confidence with interacting with him exist because we had a close relationship? Was my practice reliant on him? Had I really skilled myself up better? My colleagues on the Co-ordinator Course were very supportive and helped me to overcome my fear. So, when I first met Dylan it came quite naturally and very quickly I became more confident again.

My new project person: Dylan

I was asked to do some assessment work in relation to finding a placement for Dylan. He was staying in a respite service at the time. Corran were approached by the Multi-Disciplinary Team as they knew we practised Intensive Interaction. During the assessment, I was talking with the manager in the office when they were called away. Dylan was sat on the floor rocking and flicking a sock, so I simply sat on the floor with him and started 'talking'. With Dylan – unlike John – I felt he wanted to be with people. They both had very different life experiences. Dylan had shut himself down from people for very different reasons to John, so therefore it was fundamentally much easier to tap into Dylan than to John.

Dylan really taught me about the Tea Party Rules (Barber, 2007). We had discussed this paper and this concept in the course: the theory if you like. Dylan taught me the practice, of keeping things fluid and flexible, trying out varied responses. I think different people teach you different aspects of the practice. If you pushed a bit too far beyond Dylan's repertoire he would stop and walk away. He taught me that balance.

Now, as a manager of my services, I need to show people the way. I had to throw myself open and be vulnerable and that, psychologically, was a hard thing to do as a manager. However, I came to realise that paradoxically this has made me a better leader and a better manager.

How did you find the process of peer support and feedback on your practice during the course?

I was personally OK with this process, having a background in teaching. For me, both giving and receiving feedback felt fine. The bit I found difficult initially was learning to be quiet. This had some resonance with my style within interactions too. I would find pausing difficult, I would tend to be driving on and perhaps over-complicating things. Also, when giving feedback, I had to learn to be succinct. Watching some people struggle with this process of receiving feedback was immensely useful for helping me to understand how my staff may feel during the same process. I knew when we started to do this at work, the giving of constructive/reflective feedback would be challenging for staff.

Feedback from my course colleagues was hugely helpful in moving my practice forward. What I learned we all needed to do however, was to process that feedback. I'd go away and not realise the impact of the feedback until a month or so later. There was so much feedback within that room. The one piece of feedback that really sticks is the emotional connection my peers made with me when viewing the final video before John's death. I wasn't anticipating that others would feel the connection I had with John then. I thought it was something you would have had to be in the same room to sense. When the lights went back up I saw that many people were moved to tears and everyone was silent. I realised then how powerful video is in demonstrating II practice. I have used this video in staff training since.

Who were your mentees?

Tom is a manager in Wales and wanted to work with someone he knows very well. Initially it was quite complex. There were factors beyond my control. The young man in question has a complex diagnosis, part of which is a mental health condition and he developed a huge phobia around having the camera in the room. So, it became very difficult, if we couldn't record sessions, to track progress. My mentoring of Tom was difficult too. We were using the mentoring workbook. His practice development initially was slow. He was making all the classic mistakes that we all make at first, therefore feeling that 'it wasn't working' which resulted in him not making the commitment to it that is needed.

We had supervisions and made plans. I would come back after two weeks and he had no video footage. There were reasons given for this and we may all hear similar reasons from people who are not fully committed or on board with II. I realised, mainly by seeing other people's experience with their own mentees, that this was a confidence issue. I think Tom felt under-confident in what he was doing, particularly when being filmed. He highlighted to me that this was difficult as I was expecting him to mentor his staff team. He actually said to me, 'I feel that some of them know more than me.' That was when I made the decision that he needed to go on a course himself along with another member of staff. They have since gone on the Institute's three-day Good Practice Course. Although he had gone on the one-day course with Dave, I feel staff need more to practice well.

I stopped mentoring with Tom and his case study person. Because filming had to stop, I was concerned that this would further knock Tom's confidence. I gave him free rein to choose someone to work with and he chose Dylan. He was a little concerned that it would be too easy, but I encouraged him to stick with Dylan – the less complex interactions would give him a boost.

I was now also mentoring Donna, a relatively new member of staff. Her case study person was also new to our service. She had no previous experience of II. She was very committed to what we were doing. I was better able to express clearly what II was at this stage. Her main flaw in the beginning was that she drove on, she did too much. What she thought was that II was mostly nursery rhyme games, which she was leading. Reviewing videos together was crucial and she became addicted to doing it herself. She was very up for prolific videoing and she understood it was as much for developing her own practice as it was to capture changes in her client.

What was learnt and what progress occurred?

The course was tougher than I thought it was going to be, but in a good way. All the work I did as part of the course has been very helpful during and since in terms of developing materials for staff training.

The theoretical aspect to the course was very enjoyable. It does help enormously to know the history of the approach. The elements of the course work well together and additionally, there is your own practice development which is an on-going theme throughout the whole period. It is very useful to have videoed your starting point and where you end up. Equally, crucially, seeing other peoples' practice development was absolutely key in my own development.

Learning how to get really good quality video has helped in staff training – good video is much more effective in staff development. Learning these skills early on was crucial in getting good video footage all the way through. This has allowed staff to see subtleties in facial expressions for example. Showing feelings is difficult; showing actual concrete changes, however, is possible and crucial in convincing staff of what is happening.

What are your overall thoughts on the Co-ordinator Course and its application to Corran's services?

The course ticked the boxes that I wanted ticked but it gave me so much more that I didn't expect:

- Knowing how to mentor
- Developing my own practice
- Understanding the rationale of using II
- How to record interactions
- Technical skills – video-recording, video editing

I began using my edited films to illustrate progress within Multidisciplinary Team (MDT) meetings. I can now walk into a meeting and show one or two minutes of video and get more acknowledgement for our services and the work we do than if I had put five pages of text in front of people.

My practice development seemed to follow the same pattern of outcomes and progress in the people we support. Things moved fast and then plateaued for some time (Nind and Hewett, 2006, p.134). So too, with service development: periods of great change need to be followed by a plateauing stage of consolidation and embedding. Now, Intensive Interaction is one of the things at the forefront of my thinking whenever I plan service development.

Organisational development as a result of the course

The identification of the restraining forces was crucial in moving services forward (Lewin, 1951):

- Staff attitude/culture – II needed to have the same importance as basic care
- Lack of skills – therefore lack of knowledge around theory and confident practice of II
- Lack of leadership and ownership – so that it would carry on even when I wasn't there
- Absence of explicit mention in documents and policies.

From here I developed a strategic plan for service development. (Figure 8.1)
Tasks referred to in the diagram below:

- Tasks identified but not begun
- Partly achieved
- Fully achieved

Breaking changes down into small steps was especially important for me as I have the overall responsibility for service development and the change needed to be planned, and at a pace that was manageable. (Figure 8.2)

Every month during staff meetings and staff supervision, footage of II is shared and reviewed as part of practice development, and we use the Co-ordinator Course feedback framework. As well as developing II practice, this is a team building exercise. This enables and empowers the staff to give positive and constructive feedback about all sorts of things in other situations; it develops the language of feedback. It also develops the ability to receive praise and positive feedback. I've found that staff have more of an issue with receiving praise rather than constructive feedback! It is very true that the more we point out the positive, the less likely they will veer away from good quality interactive style. It is a bit like working with someone with challenging behaviour: don't focus on the behaviour, rather focus on everything else and develop that … the need for the behaviour will often drop away.

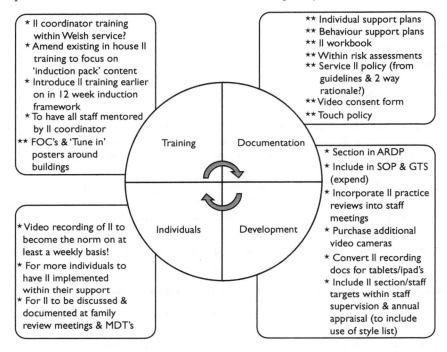

* II coordinator training within Welsh service?
* Amend existing in house II training to focus on 'induction pack' content
* Introduce II training earlier on in 12 week induction framework
* To have all staff mentored by II coordinator
** FOC's & 'Tune in' posters around buildings

** Individual support plans
** Behaviour support plans
** II workbook
** Within risk assessments
** Service II policy (from guidelines & 2 way rationale?)
** Video consent form
** Touch policy

Training

Documentation

* Section in ARDP
* Include in SOP & GTS (expend)
* Incorporate II practice reviews into staff meetings
* Purchase additional video cameras
* Convert II recording docs for tablets/ipad's
* Include II section/staff targets within staff supervision & annual appraisal (to include use of style list)

* Video recording of II to become the norm on at least a weekly basis!
* For more individuals to have II implemented within their support
* For II to be discussed & documented at family review meetings & MDT's

Individuals

Development

Figure 8.1 Strategic Plan for Service Development 1 – November 2014.

MDT - Multi Disciplinary Team
ARDP - Annual Review & Development Plan
SOP - Statement of Purpose
GTS - Guide to Services
* - Tasks identified but not begun
** - Tasks partly achieved
*** - Tasks fully achieved

Face to face mentoring is valuable, however I have found the need for regular feedback has led me to providing it in other ways rather than just face to face. So, arranging mentoring meetings via Skype and asking staff to Dropbox me video footage has enabled distance mentoring. I have completed style feedback sheets, scanned them and emailed them back to the member of staff. So, the dialogue is maintained and we avoid long periods of time without any guidance. I have been consistently surprised by how good the staff are and the progress they have made when I have stood back and 'let go' a little. This seems to increase the sense of ownership of both the approach and the progress.

I discovered through the process of looking at Lewin's theories that there was much I could do. I suddenly realised that I was 'talking the talk' and yet had not even got Intensive Interaction into our organisational aims and objectives. It wasn't in our policies and procedures;

risk assessments or care plans. If I want people to sign up to Intensive Interaction, to give it value and meaning, then I've got to give it value and meaning. It is now in all of our service documentation, from the top to the bottom. We also have videoed care plans, what someone's day might look like. We have both written (with pictures) and filmed guidelines of II with each person, with, crucially, a variety of staff using it. We have video of good practice and we have video of staff getting it wrong, the 'out-takes'! These II diaries go to the MDT meetings and are used in staff training.

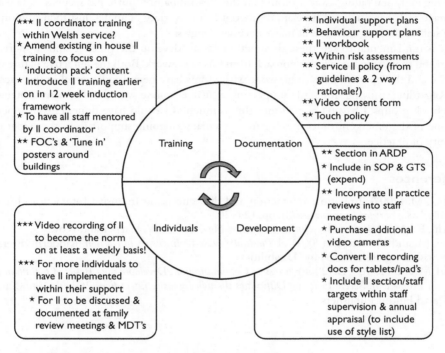

Figure 8.2 Strategic Plan for Service Development 2 - March 2015.

MDT - Multi Disciplinary Team
ARDP - Annual Review & Development Plan
SOP - Statement of Purpose
GTS - Guide to Services
* - Tasks identified but not begun
** - Tasks partly achieved
*** - Tasks fully achieved

Another crucial change I made was bringing II right to the front of staff induction training. Previously, it was a topic that came at the end after all the statutory and mandatory training. Now, it is right there at the beginning and runs all the way through. We've made the statement that II is mandatory training within Corran's services. It is in the staff contracts and job descriptions. We make it very clear that it is an expectation and that interactions will be videoed. We have now had a number of Care Managers and parents approaching us because of this level of commitment to Intensive Interaction.

What are your future plans regarding embedding II within Corran's services?

I think it is now time to re-visit, to do an audit. I know how it is here in Corran Dean. But I need to spend time at Corran Vale and see how II looks there now. I don't have a specific plan. It depends what I find and I will then respond accordingly. I want to get more people on the Good Practice course. I will revisit the development diagrams. However, it is certainly gathering pace. I have been trying to establish this for years and there has been a cycle of it sticking and then falling away. Coming on the Co-ordinator Course has secured sustainability of practice. It has stuck as I have approached it from a variety of angles. Just focussing on 'getting staff to do it' is only one of many necessary angles.

It is fundamental to see these different angles, to develop the practice and support from them and then hang the whole approach from this framework. Both the reflective nature of the course and the opportunities to network with others have been fundamental in this success.

Regarding moving forward, support is available online via the Intensive Interaction Facebook groups. I haven't tapped into this as much as I could have done. This may perhaps be one of the emergent outcomes for me – securing ongoing support from the wider community of practice.

References

Barber, M. (2007) 'Imitation, interaction and dialogue using Intensive Interaction: Tea party rules'. *Support for Learning*, 22(3). pp. 124–30.

Lewin, K. (1951) *Field Theory in Social Science*. New York, NY: Harper and Row.

Nind, M. and Hewett, D. (2001) *A Practical Guide to Intensive Interaction*. Kidderminster, UK: British Institute of Learning Disabilities.

Nind, M. and Hewett, D. (2006) *Access to Communication: Developing the Basics of Communication with People with Severe Learning Difficulties through Intensive interaction*. 2nd edn. London, UK: David Fulton Publishers.

Chapter 9

Opening the box

Accessing our ability to enjoy and understand interaction

Lucy Golder

Lucy relates her journey with Logan, and how he learnt to express his emotions to ultimately find comfort in others. The development of Intensive Interaction in her school began as an almost 'underground movement'. Lucy relates how her strength and persistence as well as the passion and dedication of other members of staff made it mainstream.

Introduction

I could start this chapter by re-iterating the infinite benefits of using Intensive Interaction, the 'fundamentals of communication' (see appendix 1) and the intended outcomes of using it as a communication method (Watson & Knight, 1991). However, there are countless literary sources of this, which put it much more succinctly than I would, and so in this chapter I am going to focus on the actualities of using Intensive Interaction in real life and the journey between you and the individual. I will also be considering ways to embark on the journey to embed Intensive Interaction into everyday life at work and especially how to implement it into a school setting as a recognised and valued communication method for our pupils.

I teach in a specialist class for children with a diagnosis of autism and severe learning difficulties within a Special school for children aged between 2 ½–11 years. The school provides education for children with profound and multiple learning difficulties, autism and severe learning difficulties. When a new school year brought a new mix of pupils, it soon became clear that one child in particular in my new class would potentially benefit immensely from Intensive Interaction – Logan.

Logan and I started our Intensive Interaction journey in September 2014. As soon as term started, it was obvious that Logan had huge communicational needs. He was currently six years old but developmentally still at a very early stage and the world appeared to be a very confusing and anxiety-inducing place to be in. His method of communication was very physical – if he was happy, he would smile or laugh and clap his hands, but this was a very self-focussed thing – he did not often attempt to engage others or seek out others to help him access the things he liked. When he was not happy he would become very distressed; he would often silently screw his face up, then begin to cry and/or scream. Often his body would go rigid (whether standing or sitting), then he would often throw himself to the floor and roll around, often hitting the ground repeatedly with his feet, hands or (less often), his head. He would also frequently pinch at his legs and body through his clothes and would mark himself quite badly. This would continue for as long as he felt it needed too. During these periods of distress, he would generally seem unaware of anyone with him and did not want to be comforted by anyone. As a team of class staff, we tried to identify some regular cause or pattern to Logan's behaviour to help us understand and support him, but we could not identify anything. Sometimes he might be thirsty, other times not, sometimes it seemed to relate to having to do something that he did not want to do, such as coming in from the playground after break, other times he would happily do whatever was asked of him. Sometimes he was happily engaged in an activity and out of the blue it happened – we could see no obvious patterns or antecedents. This type of behaviour often took up 70–80% of his school day and parents reported similar behaviours at home.

Logan

Logan had been at our school for a few years by the time he joined my class. He had always displayed these different behaviours and staff who had worked with him agreed that he was one of the most complex children they had worked with. His diagnosis is a rare gene deletion disorder – XP22.11 – which currently affects less than 20 people in the world and only two of those in this country. Logan also had autism as part of his diagnosis. Because of the rarity of his disorder, not much is known about it so we were not sure if behaviours he displayed were common to the disorder, whether they were a result of pain or discomfort he was experiencing, or as a result of environmental factors. He was very susceptible to ear infections and had previously had grommets fitted, however they did not appear to help and had been removed fairly quickly. It was also queried if he had gastrointestinal issues that caused him pain and discomfort.

It seemed plausible that this pain may be intermittent. This would mean that some days it may be low level and he would be able to cope with it. However, other days the pain may be more intense. On these days, Logan might find it difficult to cope with even familiar, everyday stimulus in addition to the intense pain he was experiencing.

The first session

My first session of Intensive Interaction with Logan was not an amazing, awe-inspiring session where a bright light bulb lit and everything clicked into place for us both!

Logan was very active and alternated between being happy and being distressed, and I was consciously aware of trying to get him to show any kind of acknowledgement that I was in the room too – not the ideal set up. Gradually, when I relaxed into the session, Logan did begin to notice me and give brief glances whilst he motored around the soft play room. When he stilled to pat the walls, I was in there and started patting with him, showing my available face. I soon realised that he was paying much more attention to my hands than my face and so I started showing him upturned 'available hands' along with my available face during inactive moments. This seemed to have a positive response and soon he was touching my hands, turning them over and exploring them. Next came clapping – Logan clapped, I clapped. When I stopped, he started taking my hands and pushing them together to make me clap. At the same time, he would very briefly glance towards my face, just once or twice. After a few minutes of this, something seemed to 'grab' Logan, he went ridgid and froze, his face silently screwed up and then the screaming began. He dropped to the ground, rolling and kicking his legs. I stayed close to him and observed, and after a few minutes he stilled and opened his eyes. I sat opposite him with my hands out and an available face. He sat up, put his head to one side and looked at me. Then he leant forward and touched my hands, vocalised, stood up and left the room, the session was finished.

I learned such a lot from this session and the available hands became a regular feature of our sessions. Having an available look is an essential aspect of the style within Intensive Interaction

(Hewett, 2012, p.47). Logan seemed indifferent to faces. He is also quite short for his age and it was quite a feat for him to look at peoples' faces, unless they made a specific effort to get down to his level. It seemed like faces confused him and that he had given up trying to decipher them. Because of this, he hardly noticed my available face and it became apparent that I needed to show my availability in other ways alongside this. I noted that Logan was very interested in hands – his and those belonging to other people. So I used my hands to show my availability for interaction. I would kneel (to be on the same level as Logan) and have my hands palm up, slightly stretched towards Logan. I would leave them there, available for him to explore and initiate interaction through touch. Often he would start by slowly turning them over and over and looking at and feeling them, then over time, he started clapping them. I added the single word 'clap!' when he started this, which brought his attention to my face; he started looking at me when I spoke and even started initiating brief moments of eye contact. Because I had my available face ready too, I would then smile at him and gradually, over time, he began to smile back. After a few weeks of this, Logan began to reach for my hands and look me in the face simultaneously. After another few weeks, his instant reaction would be to look at my face, as if 'reading' whether or not I was 'available' to him, and 'available hands' were less necessary for him. However, whenever he was distressed, I would always ensure my hands were available as in such times of anxiety, Logan preferred the security and consistency of my available hands over my available face.

The instances of distress were also becoming slightly less frequent and we even started having days with no distress at all.

The following months

Over the next few months, our Intensive Interaction sessions continued well and Logan began to initiate it at any point in the day, with a wider range of familiar adults. He even stopped a member of staff in the corridor to smile, vocalise and clap with them, on a particularly happy day! Another positive outcome of this was that Logan and I were displaying an increased understanding of each other. I had built the confidence to initially stop and observe Logan when he became distressed or very motivated, so that I could read what had caused the change in emotions and so I began to understand more about the apparent communicational intent of a lot of his behaviours. This, in turn, meant that as a staff team we were able to support Logan in far more effective ways which had the positive effect that Logan was attempting to communicate more with us in calmer ways – he seemed to feel more confident that we understood him more and were there to support him. For example, he started going into the kitchen to get a cup and then take it to an adult to indicate he needed a drink, whereas at the beginning of the term, he may have thrown himself on the floor near the kitchen and rolled around screaming. At snack time, he would eye point to the cereal he wanted and then look at the adult to indicate that he had made the decision. Our Intensive Interaction sessions continued positively. Increasingly he would be using his peripheral vision to quickly glance at me and see what I was doing and if I was watching and would interact at a moment's notice. Gradually, I lessened the amount I followed him around an area and instead stayed still in a central position. I made sure I was always facing him, had my 'available' face (and hands) and whenever he glanced at me, my face responded with a big smile, no matter how small his glance. This meant that he had to become increasingly proactive if he wanted more interaction, but equally had his space if he simply wanted to move around and smile at me from time to time, as if checking I was still there. It worked well and at times he would come over and initiate contact, give me sustained eye-contact, and move my hands to where he wanted them, e.g. his head if he wanted a head rub, or his tummy if he wanted a tickle. Sometimes he would laugh, turn his back to me and then throw himself onto me, wanting a deep squeeze. Logan was also using more vocalisations and showing an understanding of basic turn-taking by waiting and watching for my response before he continued.

A significant breakthrough happened just before Christmas 2014. Our class had gone to the hall for our physical education. session, along with another class. As it was the last but one day of term, we were having a fun session with the big parachute and music – it was busy and loud but the pupils loved it! Logan was not in a happy place though and started to cry. We got a mat out and I sat on it with him, waiting for him to initiate any interaction or communication. He immediately moved to sit close to me and put one of my hands on his right ear. I put my other hand over his other ear and he then pressed both of my hands deeper onto his ears, stopped crying and half laid down on the mat. I moved to lean on my elbow and he moved to lay on his side against me, quiet and watching the others playing. At one point, I moved my hand slightly and Logan let out a cry, looked at me and pushed my hand back against his ears. It was at this point that I realised one of his ears had started to leak a watery wax. We told his parents and a doctor's appointment confirmed that he had another ear infection. If Logan hadn't had the confidence and method of communicating that to me and I had not been so tuned into him, then it may have been much longer until the infection became apparent.

Tuning-in is an essential part of Intensive Interaction. An illustrative phrase as to how to achieve this is to 'tune in with all of your senses'. Tuning-in is when you are focussed on the pupil (or client) you are working with. You will find that the more II you do, the more subconscious this will become. It is the process of giving that person your full attention and thought; watching what they are doing, thinking about why, considering what they might do next, what they like or dislike. It is the process of 'reading' them – their body language, their communications, their actions. When you have subconsciously done this (probably within a fleeting moment!), you then respond to this. You consider your positioning in relation to the person; where they need you, where you can be best available to them. You consider your ways of responding to them; joining in, imitating, actions, vocalisations – whatever you feel at that moment is fitting, based on your knowledge from being tuned in. You instinctively assess what you are doing that is working (or not) and whether your responses are providing the best scaffolding for your pupil to explore their communication (Vygotsky, 1987). It is effective tuning-in that enables you to really get to know your pupil and begin to understand more about them. This will inevitably affect the way you work with them and plan for their learning across the whole of school life and really make their education 'person-centred'.

This confidence and understanding between Logan and other people also started to build with other members of staff. They also started to use Intensive Interaction with him and he gradually started to join in a wider range of activities in school. He still had his distressed periods, but these were generally shorter in duration and not as frequent.

Because we were getting to know Logan better, the cause of this distress was gradually becoming easier for class staff to read. We could tell more often if an outburst was mainly temper, for example; Logan did not want to do something, did not like something, or was simply in a bit of a bad mood. We could also tell at times that his outburst seemed to be a communication that there was something wrong, for example; something was painful or upsetting for him. One day in particular, this increased understanding was a very important outcome as it enabled us to identify an area that necessitated further medical investigation.

It was a Tuesday morning and our class was getting ready to go to our music session, which Logan usually quite enjoyed. However, just before we left, Logan threw himself to the ground and started to roll around, screaming and crying – it presented as if it was a temper outburst and so I stayed with him to observe, but waited for him to calm (we had identified that crowding him at these times seemed to prolong the outburst, whereas waiting for him to calm and look for a person generally meant that the outburst would stop sooner and Logan would return to the session more happily). As I was observing him, I noticed a very subtle difference that we had not seen before – his eyes were rolling up (a usual behaviour) but then seeming to fix very briefly and flicker before returning to a central position. Over the next few seconds, I continued to observe and noted that the fixed eyes also started to co-ordinate with his body going stiff, before returning to writhing and eyes moving freely. Then this became matched with an unusual high pitched scream and head banging, but when this abated, he started to look at me and make softer, distressed vocalisations. He also started reaching out for me, before he would be gripped back into the rigid phase. I called the school nurse immediately and when she saw him, we called an ambulance and his parents, as we felt that he was having some type of seizure.

When the paramedics arrived, they agreed that it seemed to be some type of seizure activity, but a few minutes after they arrived, Logan appeared to 'snap out of it' and, just like a switch had been flicked; he stood up, looked around (seeming a bit confused) and started clapping, smiling and dancing. We were all amazed at the sudden change. He was taken to the hospital and ongoing investigations began. Over the next few months, we did see this type of activity again, as did his parents at home, and investigations into possible epilepsy are ongoing. After this type of activity, Logan would also generally appear much calmer and relaxed in school for the next week or so.

The differences between this activity and his usual distressed outbursts were so minimal that I am not sure if I would have been able to identify them so swiftly if I had not grown to know Logan so well through our Intensive Interaction sessions, and had he not had a way of communicating with me. Intensive Interaction sessions help me observe and therefore tune in to the pupil so much more. It is true that both the adult and the client learn so much through Intensive Interaction – if you do not have that base of mutual understanding, confidence and respect, then it becomes much harder to understand how our pupils learn and react to the world, and it is harder for them to work out the same about the people who work with them.

The Intensive Interaction Co-ordinator Course and the mentoring process

I started the II Co-ordinator Course in 2014. My head teacher had asked if I would be interested in completing it. She had continued on to explain that because of the cost, it would have to be agreed by the school governors. Also I would have to sign an amendment to my contract; agreeing that if I left the school in the next three years, I would have to pay back the cost of the course. It was quite a commitment on both sides, but the one-day II training I had previously attended and the Intensive Interaction I had already done with pupils in school had shown me the possibilities of using the approach. I wanted to increase my depth of knowledge about it. I wanted to understand why II works, not just how to do it. I also wanted to be able to help others gain the skills and confidence to use II in their practice too, so I didn't want to pass up the opportunity!

The paperwork that came through after I had been accepted into the course was quite in depth and included information for my employer about what was required from them too, which was slightly unusual. However, after the first block, it all became clear. The course is a brilliant mix of practical and theoretical activities and perspectives. However, what you do not realise (and neither will your employer) is how much the course will actually change your outlook on a lot of areas – not just work. There should definitely be a warning for employers that at the end of the course, their employee will be a changed person with a deep belief in the essential implementation of Intensive Interaction with every child in the setting, because if we do not begin to address the 'fundamentals of communication', there is no solid base to build other learning on. And the employee will probably endeavour to do whatever they can to ensure this happens!

This determination and belief does not mean however, that the widespread implementation of Intensive Interaction is easy to achieve. That is where it is difficult because during each block of the Co-ordinator Course you are surrounded by likeminded people who support each other and help to find ways around obstacles, who share in each other's successes and support when things are hard. It's like living in an amazing Intensive Interaction bubble. Then you go back to work and it can sometimes feel like that bubble has well and truly burst – not all people share your enthusiasm or positivity about Intensive Interaction and suddenly you have so much to fit into the timetable that the task of effectively implementing it throughout your setting seems enormous. During the second half of the course, you focus on becoming a mentor to your colleagues and providing additional training, knowledge and a more in depth look at the skills and theories involved in Intensive Interaction. Initially this throws up questions such as 'who do I mentor – how do I choose?' I decided for the course to mentor one person and asked a few teachers if they would be interested. Initially I started with a teacher who unfortunately felt after a month that they didn't have the time to complete the programme and so I needed another person. Luckily another teacher was very keen and as we worked closely together in a lot of areas, it seemed a great opportunity.

At first, Nikki was understandably slightly nervous about being videoed doing Intensive Interaction but using a style sheet (see appendix 3) to help us pick out skills she was demonstrating was great to shift the emphasis from being personal to being about the skills we were observing. Nikki made a great start and seemed to tune in really well with her pupil. We discussed ways of enabling him to initiate more interactions within the setting, and Nikki tried different ways of doing things, identifying not only by the actual sessions, but also through watching her videos, things that worked and the pupil responded well to, and areas that she wanted to work on. The concept of having an 'available face' was an area we identified together as something to work on. Part of it was the nervousness of being on video, but we decided that she would try to work on making her face look more open. When we watched the next video, it was obvious that Nikki was trying hard but then a fantastic thing happened and it all fell into place. The pupil she was working with was a seven-year-old boy with almost no speech but some vocalisations. He had been making some two-syllable vocalisations, which Nikki had been imitating and he had been repeating whilst looking at her. It then became apparent that he had been rehearsing Nikki's name and then said it quite clearly 'Ni-ki', whilst really looking at her. Nikki was so excited and amazed that her face broke into a lovely smile and she visibly relaxed. Thanks to the wonders of video, we were able to rewind this and pause right on an image of her face before and then after. As soon as we had been able to physically see the difference, it clicked and Nikki has a wonderfully 'available face' now! Never underestimate the power and importance of video not just to show the progress of our pupils but also our own progress in our journey.

Once Nikki had completed the mentee programme, she became another Intensive Interaction ambassador within our setting and it was great for me to have another person who could promote the approach. Staff were also noticing that the pupils we had been working with were beginning to initiate interactions in different environments and with a wider range of people.

When they mentioned this, Nikki and I would take the opportunity to explain about the II work we had been doing and reiterate both the simplicity but effectiveness of the approach. This helped generate more interest in the mentoring programme too. However, even though the benefits of Intensive Interaction were evident for all to see and interest was being generated, actually setting up the mentoring programme within the school was not without issues. Along with this, issues of how to implement Intensive Interaction practice firmly throughout the school also became apparent.

Implementing Intensive Interaction throughout the setting

Unfortunately, as with many schools at this time of budget cuts and financial constraints, it was difficult for time to be allocated for staff or parental training in Intensive Interaction. Especially since not all staff had seen first-hand the benefits of using the approach and it was apparent that some felt it was simply another approach that either they knew about already or that they didn't have time or resources to implement in class. It is always slightly disheartening when you discover something that you feel is so essential to your pupils and it is then difficult to pass on that knowledge and passion to others. However, between Nikki and myself, people were beginning to hear about the buzz Intensive Interaction was creating and the positive effects for our pupils. Teaching Assistants (TAs) were starting to stop me in the corridor; 'Lucy, I've heard you're offering more training for Intensive Interaction, is there any chance I could …?' I explained that it would have to be in their own time and made myself available at lunchtimes and after school. Suddenly, I had two new mentees and three more who wanted to start in September! Word seemed to spread and I had soon had other professionals asking about the possibility of training, and asking if their visiting students could come and talk to me to find out more about Intensive Interaction.

So, it felt as if an almost 'underground' movement began. The Intensive Interaction Co-ordinator Course had helped me realise by this point, and accept, that there are some things you can change and some things you can't. This doesn't mean you give up on the things that you cannot change, but that you have to accept it and be creative – think outside the box about different ways of achieving your objectives. During our course, the phrase 'it is what it is' became a bit of a refrain, but it's actually very true. Don't fight battles you know you have no chance in winning, save your energy for those you can and think about ways around immovable issues. In this instance, the way around was shown by the staff coming to me and quietly asking if they could have extra Intensive Interaction training. Inadvertently this showed me that if you start the ball rolling with people who have the enthusiasm and interest to want additional training in their own time, then consequently their enthusiasm infects more people. Often, other staff around the school then begin to notice the positive changes in the pupils and start wondering what has generated these changes. At this point, you and your fellow Intensive Interaction 'converts' cannot help but to impart their knowledge and fervour of Intensive Interaction, hopefully creating more interest and curiosity about the approach, leading to a snow ball effect of more staff requesting training.

This is fairly representational of how it began in my setting. Due to budget, time and staffing constraints (as mentioned previously), the senior management were unable to allocate time during the school day to provide additional Intensive Interaction training – a common issue in many settings. This is a fairly immoveable obstacle – unless you are part of the senior management team or have some senior influence in your setting, it is unlikely that you will be able to change budget or staffing, no matter how passionate you are. So this is where you will need to think outside the box for ways around it.

In my situation the staff, their dedication and their passion gave me the way forward. They believed in II and wanted to provide the best possible opportunities for our pupils. In all honesty, the senior management were probably also quietly happy as I stopped asking for impossibilities.

Either way, this 'underground' movement that had developed was going well and towards the end of the academic year, the senior management told me the amazing news that from the following September they would be allocating half a day a week for me to dedicate to developing Intensive Interaction throughout the school. Currently, there are six members of staff who have completed the mentoring programme, nine more presently working through the programme and two more hoping to start as soon as possible – the Intensive Interaction bug is definitely infecting our school! The best change that I notice is the confidence in staff to do Intensive Interaction anywhere and anytime. It's as if their extra knowledge has enabled them to feel confident in not only what they are doing, but also why, and the opportunities that opens up for our students is amazing. It certainly makes me smile when I see a member of staff joining in with a pupil galloping down the corridor, laughing, completely tuned into them and both clearly enjoying the interaction as much as the other.

My journey so far

When I watch videos from my first few sessions of Intensive Interaction, I smile to myself at how I can see on my face that I am thinking through the things I'm doing and seem a little nervous that I might inadvertently 'get it wrong'. When I watch videos from more recent sessions, I instinctively pick out the skills and styles that I use and I am objective about what I am doing and why. I can point out what the pupils are doing, how they relate to the 'fundamentals of communication' and the progress that they are making. But a big difference is how I have become more confident and knowledgeable in my own skills so I look far more relaxed. This also has a positive effect on the pupils I work with and you can see that we are both mutually enjoying the interactions in our sessions. I feel confident that I can now 'talk the talk' as well as 'walk the walk' and I am passionate to motivate others to try Intensive Interaction, to possibly become as infected by the bug as I have, and to give our pupils/clients/friends/family of any age or any ability the best possible opportunities to develop their own interaction and communication skills that they can build on throughout the rest of their lives.

References

Hewett, D. (2012) Getting Going. In Hewett, D., Firth, G., Barber, M. and Harrison, T. (2012) *The Intensive Interaction Handbook*. London, UK: SAGE Publications. pp. 45–67.
Vygotsky, L. S. (1987) *Thinking and Speech*. New York, NY: Plenum.
Watson, J. & Knight, C. (1991) 'An evaluation of intensive interaction teaching with pupils with very severe learning difficulties', *Child Language Teaching and Therapy*, 7(3), pp. 310–325.

Chapter 10

Intensive Interaction
From Einstein to Lady Gaga

Ben Smith

Ben outlines how Intensive Interaction made him re-evaluate and change his practice from one focussing on behavioural modification to one focussing on relationships and emotional well-being. His biggest learning opportunity was presented to him under the name of Mick, and Ben recalls how he had to learn to do less, in order to let Mick do more.

Introduction and some service history

This is the story of a personal journey from 'directiveness' to 'responsiveness'. Learning how to socially and emotionally connect and interact more effectively with intellectually disabled people at the earliest stages of communicative ability has enabled them to progress better with learning the 'fundamentals of communication' (see appendix 1).

My name is Ben Smith. I am now 51 years of age and although chronologically mature, I, like many, still feel reasonably young at heart and despite my advancing years, still feel that 'every day is a school day' in terms of learning new things. Originally, a purveyor of quality, preowned automobiles (yes, a second-hand car salesman!), I have been employed in the Specialist Psychology and Behavioural Services of Hywel Dda University Health Board's Learning Disabilities Service in South West Wales for nearly 25 years. Over that time, my work with intellectually disabled individuals whose behaviour presents a challenge to others, has predominantly focussed on three key areas:

- Behaviour modification via reinforcement and incentive-based approaches.
- Behaviour management via antecedent (trigger) prevention and reactive physical intervention techniques.
- Total communication approaches including signs, symbols (PECS, or picture exchange communication system), objects and simplified key word language.

In addition to these key areas, I have attended a plethora of training events devoted to approaches aimed at intervening with children and adults with intellectual disabilities such as PBS (Positive Behavioural Support), TEACCH (Treatment and Education of Autistic and Communication Handicapped Children), SRV (Social Role Valorisation), Active Support, Gentle Teaching, Systematic Instruction, etc. My role as a behaviour specialist over the years has focussed on trying to find solutions to address a whole range of behavioural challenges exhibited by a huge variety of incredibly interesting people. At the centre of this work has always been the accepted philosophy that behavioural problems displayed by people with intellectual disabilities are rooted in communication deficits and the principle of teaching functional alternatives to challenging behaviours has been paramount.

However, all too often, the needs of the 'system' for rapid solutions and effective management strategies for carers seem to heavily influence the advice provided. In my experience, such situational management advice based upon identifying and removing known 'triggers' for challenging behaviour can often be found to inadvertently reinforce the problem behaviour. For example, many behaviour management plans suggest reducing or removing demands in response to identified problematic behaviours as a strategy for reducing the 'target' behaviour. All very well you might say, but in many cases and in the absence of any parallel approaches to teach or develop the individual's communication abilities, this can often serve to simply strengthen the need for the individual to behave in this manner to avoid the unpleasant experience of being demanded to engage in non-preferred activities or tasks which in turn, are actually often poorly matched to their abilities and developmental level.

Surely, giving regard to and adjusting the level of and nature of demands present within the environment would be much more beneficial to all. In some instances, I have even been asked to implement interventions that 'help' or 'encourage' individuals to better tolerate or cope with the demands that their lifestyles present them with! Even in apparent person-centred care cultures, this has often left me questioning the true beneficiaries of such 'programmes'. That is to say, that utilising often powerful reinforcers and incentives to get 'control' over or suppress other human being's behaviour in order to attain participation and activity engagement goals or 'better quality of life' feels somewhat adrift of the core values statements of many service or care providers. This has all left me querying whether the objectives for my current role are more aimed at achieving a specific percentage of reduction or suppression of a given challenging behaviour, rather than a concern with the emergence of a better developed, more competent and contented individual.

Whilst having experienced some degree of 'success' with the former in reducing some individual's problematic behaviours, I have often felt that I have been missing something crucial about the inner person and the inner person's needs. However, the clinical culture I work within hasn't seemed to encourage, or require any alternative approaches. Fortunately, my role gives me some responsibility to influence that. Without the experience of participating in the Co-ordinator's Course, I would probably never have questioned the approaches I adopted and continued to 'bang my head against the wall' in the quest for success. This reminds me of the famous (allegedly) Albert Einstein quote on insanity, which he defined as:

> *'Continuing to repeat the same processes to address the same problems and expecting different outcomes each time!'*

Having been inspired by the work of Dave Hewett over the years and having had the good fortune to attend his one-day Intensive Interaction workshop with almost serial regularity, I felt privileged to say the least, when he encouraged me to consider attending his Co-ordinator's Course. My journey began with much discussion and pleading to my superiors in the University Health Board to consider funding this. With some support, I then proceeded to negotiate 50 per cent of the course fees from our partner organisation, the Local Social Services Authority on the grounds of 'joint initiative'. This was no mean feat but thankfully it was eventually agreed. However, final approval was not actually given until I was halfway from West Wales to Malvern in Worcestershire for the first day of the course! I remember well, the moment my text notification sounded and I looked across at the screen and saw the words 'it's approved Ben, you can go!'

The delay in getting the funding approved for my course until the eleventh hour meant that I had not been able to prepare for the course in quite the same manner as some of my fellow budding Co-ordinators. The course typically requires preparatory work that I had not undertaken and I remember feeling rather unprepared and inadequate. This was compounded further when I saw the video evidence of what my peers were capable of, even at the beginning of the course. But, masking anxiety is something that I've worked hard at over the years and with handouts and borrowed video camera to hand, I embarked on a journey of learning and self-reflection that would completely reshape my thinking and practice. The story of this journey will hopefully influence readers to consider making a similar one themselves.

Mick and I

As soon as I returned from my first training block, fully inspired yet again, I began the process of identifying a suitable 'victim' (communication partner) with which to apply my learning. Running an Intensive Interaction project within a workplace, mentoring the staff, shooting videos, are all part of the course. I had already identified a service where I had thought a number of individuals would benefit from Intensive Interaction, so I went along and undertook some observations. I recall sitting at the table in the dining room and observing several individuals but have to admit feeling rather 'godlike' with my selection thoughts. That is, which one of these beautiful, interesting folks shall I pick to hopefully improve the quality of their life? It had been suggested by the facilitators on the course that one should avoid selecting someone with highly complex needs and presentation at this early stage of our learning.

Taking that advice into consideration, I began to judge people's complexity in my mind and the process became more and more difficult. Just at that moment, I glanced across the table to the gentleman who sat on the end of it, eating his lunch. My glance turned into a prolonged gaze and then Mick looked at me with a somehow 'knowing' look that seemed to say 'Go on, pick me!' I employed a warm and welcoming facial expression to respond to his extended, fixed stare and he seemed to acknowledge my presence and the look on my face briefly, before diverting his attention back to his dinner plate! This seemed enough for me, so I began to quiz his carers for information about his range of needs and abilities. Mick seemed, and was described by his carers, as such a quiet chap with very few communicative actions or intentions. This results in him being very socially isolated, even in his busy day service environment.

Discussions with his family revealed that in his very early years he had appeared to show some progress with communication development in using vocalisations and some poorly formed words but this had not been sustained and he had remained fairly consistent with his current range of needs and abilities from the age of about three. He has no verbal language but does apparently know the sign, or at the least a version in his own dialect for 'toilet'. It is perhaps not surprising therefore, that much of his experience of communication must have been directive towards him. His receptive language seemed quite good in so much as he could respond to verbal instructions, although I suspect that only when these directions, commands and demands are of a type he had developed an understanding of through repetition or routine e.g., come and get a drink, get your coat, come for dinner, get on the bus, etc. All this suggested that Intensive Interaction would help me to begin connecting with and getting to know Mick while slowly enabling him to get more enjoyment out of being with others.

I arrived for my first session, and set about just being in Mick's company and attempting to observe him for behaviour and communication attempts that I could respond to. As my fellow course participants later pointed out, I think I was nonetheless overdoing things somewhat. In fact, Mick seemed rather overwhelmed by my attempts to interact with him and in a delight-fully honest fashion he simply turned his back on me and began to twirl his hair. Over time, I realised with a little help from Mick and my peers, that 'less is more' in Intensive Interaction and the first obstacle was for me to try and get control of my own behaviour and communi-cation excesses before I stood a chance of allowing Mick to get in the communication driv-ing seat. This is the sense of 'minimalism' we were learning about on the course, part of the essence of Intensive Interaction. Less is more. Learn to hold back the mass of your complicated behaviour so that the other person has time and space in which to operate, to find out how to initiate, then gradually how to positively work *you* with their behaviour. Over and over again in videos of successful Intensive Interactions on our course days, we would discuss this visible, simple secret of not doing too much, waiting, waiting for the other person's initiations and building the activity by responding to them.

I began to realise just how difficult this can be and during these challenging times, I reflected rather depressingly on how many other individuals at the earliest stages of communication I must have 'blown away' with my exuberance over the last 25 years of work in this field. But, with my 'every day's a school day' attitude, I began to see Mick as often as I could and with warm constructive and reflective feedback from the course cohorts and facilitators, I began to make progress with what turned out to be equally as much my journey as Mick's.

The environment Mick spends his days in is a busy activity centre and it seemed fairly clear that not many people have the time to spend with him doing what I was doing. Like so many individuals who have yet to develop challenging behaviour as a result of significant commu-nication impairments, the assessment of their needs never seems to identify adequate intensive support to address this. It is even more unlikely that this communication need is prioritised in their care plans. This should be worthy of note to any readers with responsibility for assessing people's needs. I got the distinct impression sometimes that Mick almost seemed to be think-ing I was going to leave him at any time soon, as this may have been a typical experience for him. He almost seemed surprised and intrigued by my continued presence as if to say, 'nobody normally stays around this long!' I liked this thought and it helped me a lot in maintaining my slower, patient, more responsive approach.

Over the weeks and months, Mick seemed to become far more accepting of my company. On occasions, he actually appeared to acknowledge my arrival into his space by shifting in his seat as if to prepare himself for time we spent together. I remember thinking about the impor-tance and value of repetition in influencing familiarity. These tiny, surely significant changes were worthy of recognition given my earlier experiences with him and I duly recorded them on his Progress Track (see appendix 4) and pointed them out to his carers and anyone else who would listen! I now felt more confident that my efforts were having some genuinely positive effect on our relationship and simply just in terms of consent, his shifting towards me rather than turning away, felt hugely important.

My work commitments meant that the sessions with Mick weren't always easy to plan and became irregular as a result. I experienced a sense of having to start again sometimes or at least a few paces back from where I had left off the previous time. This is an important point of note for practitioners. I also learnt that in my attempts to 'resume' our 'conversation' I often did too much in terms of my responses and I recall reflecting on how easy it is to take relationships for granted based on limited positive experiences. Thus, it became apparent that I somehow had to earn the right to progress with Mick. I thought this gave him a great amount of control and was something that I doubt he has had much of in his life. On the subject of control, getting control of my own communication behaviour was probably the most difficult thing to do for my Intensive Interaction practice. However, as my awareness of this need increased and I was rewarded for it by magic communication moments, it began to get easier and more natural and this development of my practitioner skill was remarked upon by my peers during the video evaluation element of every training block.

Intensive Interaction practitioners know that things can take time. These new developments we are going for, they can seem like a really big deal for someone like Mick. As he makes progress, he is actually undertaking a life transformation in his everyday experience and indeed, three months into our journey, I started to become regularly rewarded by the comments of Mick's carers who reported on their observations of him at other times. They said things like 'Mick seems so much more sociable now' and 'Mick seems much more willing to join in with our activities'. This felt good and important as Mick had seemed so socially isolated before despite his presence in the social environment.

Mentoring

With some of his carers showing such interest in the work that I was doing and reporting on the outcomes, the mentoring element of the Co-ordinator's Course seemed to become highly relevant. Obviously, for Mick to truly benefit from Intensive Interaction, more input than my episodic visits were needed. In any event, bringing on other members of staff is an aspect of one's project within the course.

In fact, most carers in Mick's day service had themselves been on a one-day workshop that the organisation had commissioned from the Intensive Interaction Institute, delivered by Dave Hewett. There seemed to be a genuine appetite for Intensive Interaction at all levels within the organisation and much of this was often visible during the time I spent at the service. There was an eagerness to talk to me about their experiences and in fact some of this eagerness to engage me in conversation about the approach and their experiences sometimes further impeded my ability to engage with Mick!

So, with my mentee Donna, identified through a process of natural selection, I began the highly enjoyable task of shaping her technical style by adopting the 'video evaluation' approach that had proved so useful and beneficial for my own practice. When we had overcome the, I expect often typical, anxiety that people seem to experience when seeing themselves on film, this mentoring process proved highly fruitful in terms of developing the relationship that Donna also had with Mick. This was already a positive relationship given her delightfully bubbly and amiable manner with the individuals in her care but I think she, like I had done, recognised through video evaluation and reflective practice that she could achieve much greater connection through simply 'being with' Mick and adopting a more responsive approach to his subtle communication attempts.

Having said that, we did record some special moments during a shared activity of blowing bubbles and this particular activity seemed to offer a rather enjoyable and relaxing 'vehicle' to sharing space where they rehearsed turn taking, eye contact exchanges and anticipation 'play' that had rarely, if at all, been observed and enjoyed with Mick before. Donna began to acknowledge her own practice development and despite the occasional gentle use of practical activity, began to understand the significance and relevance of my suggestion that this might be due to us being human 'beings' not human 'doings'! That is to say, that simply 'being with' each other has equal if not more significance than 'doing things' with each other and if the 'being with' is done well, it can be immensely mutually satisfying and pleasurable.

With increasing expectation of my developing skills, my managers and fellow professional communication colleagues began to identify other settings for me to try and apply my knowledge and mentoring skills and I began visiting a local authority day service setting for people with intellectual disabilities, many of whom were profoundly disabled and seemingly prime candidates for Intensive Interaction approaches. I was introduced to Theresa, who had been identified by the service as someone who, having been on Dave Hewett's one-day course could co-ordinate the implementation of the approach within the service. Theresa is a wonderful person with natural warmth and enthusiasm for anything that she feels will benefit the people she cares for. But, by her own admission, she lacked confidence of her own abilities. We started working together and through discussion and video evaluation I watched her gain in confidence and begin to demonstrate some magnificent Intensive Interaction technique much of which she, in rather typical Theresa fashion, attributed to me and the support I offered her. I watched her develop into a competent practitioner and this felt highly rewarding, as too were the emerging outcomes for the individual who was the focus of our attentions.

Inspiration is a powerful motivator of intention and practice. It is a word I have seen often used by attendees of Dave Hewett's Intensive Interaction workshops to capture feelings as participants leave to embark on their own practice journeys. I too, began to feel that my mentees felt more inspired following our sessions together and were recognising and crucially enjoying the value of working with the people in their care in this 'new' way. With each visit, I began to see evidence of this recognition filtering into the attitudes and values of the wider care teams in both settings and this felt good.

Overall I was feeling rather pleased with my progress to date but with so many positives arising out of my participation on the Co-ordinator's Course, I suppose being realistic, something had to balance that out and in a rather uncanny fashion, just at the point that the course block entitled 'working with staff groups' was scheduled, my mentees and I began to encounter some apathy and sort of resistance to our attempts to embed Intensive Interaction approaches into the respective service settings we were operating in. In light of the initial enthusiasm and appetite for the approach, I suppose I was surprised and a little disappointed by this. In my experience in behavioural services, I had encountered innovation decay before and was therefore all too aware that it can be difficult to introduce new ideas and ways of working into any group and sustain them, even when outcomes seem positive. However, I suppose I thought the inherent simplicity of Intensive Interaction and the video evidence of what was possible, ought to make things more sustainable. Such innovation decay can often be addressed through the provision of regular stimulus and in this case this seemed to highlight the value of the role of Co-ordinator. The inclusion within the Co-ordinator's Course itinerary of a session dedicated to methods of addressing this issue was of great reassurance that it had been encountered before over the years and therefore, might be considered expected to some degree and importantly, I probably wasn't solely responsible!

Given my experiences in the behavioural field, I found the 'Working with Staff Groups' training block really helpful and on my return to the workplace set about undertaking my 'Restraining Forces' (Lewin, 1951) project with the staff teams I was working with. The approaches suggested by the facilitators and also my co-participants (who had also encountered similar issues) really helped with attending to some of the obstacles I was encountering and definitely seemed to aid bringing things back on track. The analogy I considered at this time was 'plate spinning'. In other words, in order to avoid to the plates wobbling and falling off the spikes, you have to keep attending to them and giving them a spin with a sort of reliable consistency and I considered how this plate spinning is the very kind of stimulus that the role of an Intensive Interaction Co-ordinator can bring to the lives of those who benefit most from this approach.

Reflections

So, what had I learnt by attending the Co-ordinator's Course? Well, I reflected on the realisation that the beauty and wonder of communication has far greater depth than the functional communication skills that tend to be focussed on when teaching or 'conditioning' in the field of intellectual disability. Whilst functional communication clearly has a value in helping people communicate their basic needs and wants, much of this continues to be delivered in a rather directive fashion by bombarding the individual with often demanding instructions and does little to enhance access to the 'real person' and the development of better quality relationships.

Also, while the outcomes associated with the suppression of problematic behaviours through modification methods seem to be perceived as improving quality of life by many services, does it really encourage the naturalistic development of psychologically and emotionally contented people? I fear not, and despite the seemingly great philosophical strides made in disabled people's status and role in society, perhaps until we can truly and fully address some of these fundamental issues relating to human well-being then I feel that we may have failed this population.

My own personal learning experience through attendance in the Co-ordinator's Course is by far, the most beneficial I have encountered in my career. I completely underestimated the potential for this at the point of signing up. It prompted me to closely examine my own views and values and has been highly influential in shifting my well-established attitudes and beliefs regarding the population of folks with intellectual disabilities. The outcome has been so significant that it has since prompted me to endeavour pursuing an alternative role within my employing organisation which truly excites me. The Co-ordinators Course content and its delivery by hugely experienced and talented facilitators seemed to encourage the participants' learning to emerge at their own pace rather than be forced in any way. I often pondered the similarity between this naturally emerging outcome and the outcomes that are possible from Intensive Interaction practice itself. The course substance and discussion takes the learner on a journey from historical approaches and attitudes relating to intellectual disabilities and autism through a range of theoretical perspectives to enable the learner to draw their own conclusions while debating, challenging and rethinking one's previously held views and beliefs and this seems rather unique in this field where all too often training in specific approaches seems to be delivered in a rather 'This is the only way' style.

One key area of change in my thinking from now on is giving greater respect to and acknowledgement of, an individual's developmental stage and abilities communicatively, emotionally, psychologically and behaviourally. This, for me highlighted 'our' collective responsibility to create caring and learning environments more pertinent to developmental stages in which individuals are then better enabled to connect with and relate to those around them. The development of more meaningful reciprocal relationships will facilitate their progress with learning fundamental communication and social skills in a naturalistic way that can help them begin to overcome the challenges they face in acquiring the best possible quality of life.

Although based on a thorough understanding of the theoretical basis for human communication and development, the simplicity of Intensive Interaction surely makes it one of the most naturally achievable approaches ever described. This concept too, reminds me of the quote incorrectly attributed again to Albert Einstein. It was actually Schumacher (1973) who said:

> 'Any intelligent fool can make things bigger and more complex, but it takes a touch of genius and a lot of courage to go in the other direction.'

For me, this just sits very well in my thoughts regarding the approach and perhaps could be given greater thought in many aspects of human services.

With every passing block of the course, my mind became more settled and my lone journeys home gave me the chance to reflect on my learning and changes in my thinking. At times this was so powerful, that upon my return to work, I often felt rather isolated due to working with colleagues that did not appear to initially share or fully appreciate my newly acquired views! I recall describing my experience analogously to some as if I had been on a life changing 'tour of duty' similar to military service in Afghanistan or Vietnam where few understood the person-changing events and experiences that occurred and it was therefore very difficult to talk about it to those not involved. This soon passed though, as I developed my ability to talk about my perspectives in my own way and begin the task of trying to shape or influence others' views to align with my own that I felt would benefit those we work with and support day to day.

Somehow words alone don't seem adequate to fully convey the pleasure and educational value of the course experience, much of which actually came from my fellow participants. We all shared a passion for Intensive Interaction but brought a variety of backgrounds, cultures, life and career experiences to this place and I recall thinking that the individuals fortunate enough to have these, let's face it 'paid' people in their lives, were truly in safe and competent hands. The videos I watched with envy on the first block continued to gladden my heart from block to block as I watched my peers' skills develop. However, I recall thinking frequently that these gradual refinements to each individual's practice, were only really adding shine to what were already, highly polished individuals in my eyes and to share this company regularly could only be beneficial for me personally.

The final block and 'graduation' duly arrived, far too quickly for me if I remember correctly and we all arrived in Malvern to present our work. Some or indeed all, of the other participant's practice that I had seen along the way during video evaluation exercises once again resulted in a great deal of anxiety on my part as to the quality of my own project in terms of both technique and outcomes. By this time though, the nurturing and supportive manner in which the facilitators and my peers had helped me develop, left me reasonably confident that all would be well. We set up the equipment and began to volunteer our turn. What followed was a truly moving few days of watching superbly edited video diaries of each selected individual's progress depicting the development of the 'fundamentals of communication' and the visibly obvious growth and blossoming of the relationship between those individuals and their Intensive Interaction partner. The addition of a soundtrack to some of the video stories brought tears to mine and many other's eyes and once again, I reflected repeatedly on the priceless value of this approach in terms of quality of life. Our certificates were awarded and we all gathered for a final 'Big Thought'. Many emotional words were exchanged that afternoon and there was a tinge of sadness that our journeys had come to some sort of an end as most do. I think I can speak on behalf of all of us though, in saying that they were only really just beginning and I left the group with what I thought a rather fitting quote that many in the group believed to be from some historical prophet, but that was actually Lady Gaga:

'If you have revolutionary potential, you have a moral obligation to make the world a better place.'

I have no doubt whatsoever, that the remarkable human beings that attended Malvern 7 in 2014/15 will certainly fulfil this prophecy and I dedicate this story to them all.

References

Lewin, K. (1951) *Field Theory in Social Science.* New York, NY: Harper and Row.
Schumacher, E.F. (1973) 'Small is Beautiful'. *The Radical Humanist*, 37(5). pp. 22.

The fundamentals of communication

- Enjoying being with another person
- Developing the ability to attend to that person
- Concentration and attention span
- Learning to do sequences of activity with another person
- Taking turns in exchanges of behaviour
- Sharing personal space
- Using and understanding eye contact
- Using and understanding facial expressions
- Using and understanding physical contacts
- Using and understanding non-verbal communication
- Using vocalisations with meaning
- Learning to regulate and control arousal levels

The fundamentals of communication 2
Emotional learning

- Knowing that others care, learning to care
- Enjoying being with another person – connecting, bonding, etc
- Attachment, attunement
- Self-security, to feel safe, secure, calm
- Self-esteem, sense of self
- To identify own feelings & see same in others
- Gradually to understand feelings
- Trust stuff, etc.
- Empathy, knowing/caring about how somebody else feels
- Right-hemisphere brain development (early emotional learning prepares areas of the brain for later, higher functions)

(based on various: Bowlby et al., 1953, Lamb et al, 2002, Schore, 2003)

Style / technique list

Video:	
Available look	
Available self / body	
Positioning	
Observes	
Tunes in	
Relaxed	
Enjoyment	
Unhurried	
Does not drive on	
Pauses	
Waits	
Doesn't do too much	
Responsive	
Timing / tempo / pace / flow	
Ways of responding	
Responds to vocalisations	
Responds with running commentary	
Joins in	
Imitates	
Use of touch	
Finds the right moment to develop, build, extend	
Uses scenario 2 when right	
Anything else? Comments	

Progress track

Progress Track for:	Date started:		1 2 3 4 5 6 7 8 9 10 11 12 13 14 15 16 17 18 19 20 21 22 23 24 25 26 27 28 29 30 31

Index